I0415728

May 2012

TROUBLED ASSET RELIEF PROGRAM

Government's Exposure to AIG Lessens as Equity Investments Are Sold

GAO

Accountability ★ Integrity ★ Reliability

GAO-12-574

May 2012

TROUBLED ASSET RELIEF PROGRAM

Government's Exposure to AIG Lessens as Equity Investments Are Sold

Why GAO Did This Study

Assistance provided by Treasury under the Troubled Asset Relief Program (TARP) and by the Federal Reserve to AIG represented one of the federal government's largest investments in a private-sector institution. AIG is a holding company that, through its subsidiaries, engages in a broad range of insurance and insurance-related activities in the United States and abroad.

As part of GAO's statutory oversight of TARP, this report updates a set of indicators GAO last reported in July 2011. Specifically, GAO discusses (1) the status of the government's exposure to AIG and (2) trends in the financial condition of AIG and its insurance companies. To update the indicators, GAO primarily used available public filings as of December 31, 2011, and other publicly available information as of March 31, 2012; reviewed rating agencies' reports; and identified critical activities and discussed them with relevant agency officials.

Treasury, the Federal Reserve, and AIG provided technical comments that GAO incorporated, as appropriate.

View GAO-12-574. For more information, contact Lawrance L. Evans at (202) 512-4802 or evansl@gao.gov.

What GAO Found

Since GAO's last report in July 2011, more of the assistance provided by the Department of the Treasury (Treasury) and the Board of Governors of the Federal Reserve System (Federal Reserve) to benefit American International Group, Inc. (AIG) has been repaid. As of March 22, 2012, the remaining assistance to AIG was $46.3 billion, including unpaid dividends and accrued interest. This amount includes Treasury's $35.9 billion investment in AIG common stock and a balance of $8.3 billion owed by Maiden Lane III to the Federal Reserve Bank of New York (FRBNY). This remaining assistance was down from $92.5 billion in March 2011 and $154.7 billion in December 2010. Several indicators show that as of March 2012, the government's remaining outstanding assistance to AIG has continued to be reduced, mostly because of repayments on the FRBNY loan to Maiden Lane II; repayment of AIA Aurora, LLC, a special purpose vehicle; and sales of Treasury's common stock in AIG. The government's outstanding assistance to AIG is largely composed of Treasury's common stock in AIG. Treasury's sales of AIG stock in May 2011 and March 2012 have yielded total proceeds of $11.8 billion and reduced Treasury's ownership to 70 percent of the company. Based on the $30.83 closing share price of AIG common stock on March 30, 2012, Treasury could recoup the total value of assistance extended to AIG and take in an additional $2.7 billion including dividends. The remaining assistance through Maiden Lane III will likely be repaid in full and net additional returns to the government. When all the assistance is considered, the amount the federal government ultimately takes in could exceed the total support extended to AIG by more than $15.1 billion. This analysis is primarily based on repayments and recoveries and market valuation of AIG's stock and does not include estimates of subsidy costs associated with the assistance. The actual repayment of the remaining assistance continues to depend on AIG's long-term health, the timing of Treasury's sale and the share price of AIG stock, among other things. As Treasury arranges to sell its stock in AIG to exit the company, several indicators suggest that the most likely buyers will be institutions, many of whom already have considerable holdings in other insurance companies.

Several indicators show that in 2011, AIG had positive net income and its insurance operations were stable and profitable. AIG had a net income for 2011 of $18.5 billion, primarily attributable to an income tax benefit and divested businesses. AIG's operating cash flows declined in 2011, which was mostly due to cash payments covering several years of accrued interest and fees on the FRBNY revolving credit facility and reduction in cash flows from the absence of a full year of operating cash flows of foreign life subsidiaries that were sold during the year. Also, payments on catastrophic loss claims and asbestos liabilities reduced operating cash flows. The indicator on AIG's quarterly insurance operating performance shows that AIG was profitable in most quarters and that investment income contributed considerably to that profitability, including several quarters when insurance underwriting by itself was not profitable. The sustainability of any positive trends in AIG's operations will depend on how well it manages its business in the current economic environment. GAO will continue to monitor these issues.

Contents

Abbreviations

AIA	AIA Group Limited
AIG	American International Group, Inc.
AIGFP	AIG Financial Products Corp.
ALICO	American Life Insurance Company
CDO	collateralized debt obligation
CDS	credit default swap
DPW	direct premiums written
EESA	Emergency Economic Stabilization Act of 2008
Federal Reserve	Board of Governors of the Federal Reserve System
FRBNY	Federal Reserve Bank of New York
RMBS	residential mortgage-backed security
S&P	Standard & Poor's
SBF	securities borrowing facility
SEC	Securities and Exchange Commission
SIGTARP	Special Inspector General for TARP
SPV	special purpose vehicle
TARP	Troubled Asset Relief Program
Treasury	Department of the Treasury

May 7, 2012

Congressional Committees

Assistance provided to American International Group, Inc., (AIG) has represented one of the federal government's largest investments in a private-sector institution. AIG is a holding company that through its subsidiaries engages in a broad range of insurance and insurance-related activities in the United States and abroad, including property/casualty insurance, life insurance and retirement services, mortgage guaranty, aircraft leasing, financial services, and asset management. Its potential demise in 2008 threatened to further disrupt the already troubled financial markets. To minimize the likelihood of such a scenario, the Board of Governors of the Federal Reserve System (Federal Reserve) and, subsequently, the Department of the Treasury (Treasury) deemed AIG to be systemically significant, opening the door for these entities to provide extraordinary assistance to AIG. The Federal Reserve, through its emergency powers under section 13(3) of the Federal Reserve Act, and Treasury, through the Emergency Economic Stabilization Act of 2008 (EESA), which authorized the Troubled Asset Relief Program (TARP), collaborated to make available more than $180 billion for the benefit of AIG.[1] This assistance has been used to strengthen AIG's financial condition and avert the company's failure and, in turn, further disruption of the financial markets. Since January 2011, when AIG, the Federal Reserve, and Treasury took steps to recapitalize AIG, the company has continued repayment of its federal assistance. The extent to which Treasury will further recoup its investment will continue to depend on the long-term health of AIG and a number of other factors. Under our statutorily mandated responsibilities for providing timely oversight of

---

[1] EESA, Pub. L. No. 110-343, 122 Stat. 3765 (2008), codified at 12 U.S.C. §§ 5201 et seq. EESA originally authorized Treasury to purchase or guarantee up to $700 billion in troubled assets. The Helping Families Save Their Homes Act of 2009, Pub. L. No. 111-22, Div. A, 123 Stat. 1632 (2009), amended EESA to reduce the maximum allowable amount of outstanding troubled assets under the act by almost $1.3 billion, from $700 billion to $698.741 billion. While the Secretary of the Treasury extended the authority provided under EESA through October 3, 2010, the Dodd-Frank Wall Street Reform and Consumer Protection Act, Pub. L. No. 111-203, 124 Stat. 1376 (2010), enacted on July 21, 2010, (1) reduced Treasury's authority to purchase or insure troubled assets to $475 billion and (2) prohibited Treasury from using its authority under EESA to incur any additional obligations for a program or initiative unless the program or initiative already had begun before June 25, 2010.

TARP, we are continuing to report on the federal government's assistance to AIG.[2]

To help Congress monitor the condition of AIG and the government's ability to recoup its assistance to AIG, we have developed indicators to monitor the status of the government's exposure to AIG and trends in AIG's financial condition. Because government assistance to AIG is a coordinated approach, in addition to providing timely reporting of Treasury's assistance to AIG, we are also monitoring the efforts of the Federal Reserve.[3] In September 2009 we issued a report on the financial condition and the status of government's exposure to AIG in which we first reported on these indicators. Since then, we have continued to monitor the financial risk posed by AIG, its financial condition, and the status of its repayment efforts.[4] This report provides an update on the AIG indicators primarily based on AIG's latest available public filings as of

---

[2]We must report at least every 60 days on findings resulting from oversight of TARP's performance in meeting the purposes of EESA, the financial condition and internal controls of TARP, the characteristics of both asset purchases and the disposition of assets acquired, TARP's efficiency in using the funds appropriated for the program's operation, TARP's compliance with applicable laws and regulations, and other matters. 12 U.S.C. § 5226(a).

[3]Our ability to review the Federal Reserve's assistance was clarified by the Helping Families Save Their Homes Act of 2009, enacted on May 20, 2009, which provided us authority to audit Federal Reserve actions taken under section 13(3) of the Federal Reserve Act "with respect to a single and specific partnership or corporation." Among other things, this amendment provides us with authority to audit Federal Reserve actions taken for three entities also assisted under TARP—Citigroup, Inc.; AIG; and the Bank of America Corporation. It also gives us the authority to access information from entities participating in TARP programs, such as AIG, for purposes of reviewing the performance of TARP. Section 1109 of the Dodd-Frank Wall Street Reform and Consumer Protection Act provided us authority to review various aspects of Federal Reserve facilities initiated in response to the financial crisis.

[4]See GAO, *Troubled Asset Relief Program: The Government's Exposure to AIG Following the Company's Recapitalization*, GAO-11-716 (Washington, D.C.: July 18, 2011); *Troubled Asset Relief Program: Third Quarter 2010 Update of Government Assistance Provided to AIG and Description of Recent Execution of Recapitalization Plan*, GAO-11-46 (Washington, D.C.: Jan. 20, 2011); and *Troubled Asset Relief Program: Status of Government Assistance to AIG*, GAO-09-975 (Washington, D.C.: Sept. 21, 2009). For our previous testimony on the assistance provided to AIG, see *Troubled Asset Relief Program: Update of Government Assistance Provided to AIG*, GAO-10-475 (Washington, D.C.: Apr. 27, 2010), and *Federal Financial Assistance: Preliminary Observations on Assistance Provided to AIG*, GAO-09-490T (Washington, D.C.: Mar. 18, 2009). For our review of the assistance offered by the Federal Reserve to AIG, see *Financial Crisis: Review of Federal Reserve Financial System Assistance American International Group, Inc.*, GAO-11-616 (Washington, D.C.: Sept. 30, 2011).

December 31, 2011, and other more recent publicly available information where available. Specifically, the report discusses (1) the status of the government's exposure to AIG and (2) trends in the financial condition of AIG and its insurance companies.

To conduct this work, we updated previously published indicators that address several dimensions of AIG's business. Data used to create the indicators were collected from several sources, but most were based on publicly available information, such as AIG's 10K and 10Q filings with the Securities and Exchange Commission (SEC) and insurance regulatory filings with the respective states of domicile (copies of which were provided to the National Association of Insurance Commissioners). We analyzed AIG's SEC filings and supplements for those filings through the fourth quarter of 2011. We analyzed data from Thomson Reuters Datastream, SNL Financial, and Yahoo Finance.com. We obtained the ratings data of AIG from credit rating agencies. We also analyzed data from recent issues of the Federal Reserve weekly statistical releases H.4.1 and Treasury 105(a) and transaction reports.

To monitor the status of the government's exposure to AIG, we updated some indicators, excluded others, and developed several new ones. We updated and revised our indicators of the composition of the government's assistance to AIG to more broadly include all of the Federal Reserve Bank of New York (FRBNY) and Treasury assistance that has been provided to AIG since 2008. We did not include our indicator that focused on the composition and level of the government's direct assistance to AIG before and upon announcement and execution of the recapitalization agreement because another new indicator provides a longer historical perspective on the level and composition of all government assistance to, and on behalf of, AIG. In addition, we have added several new indicators to track the status of the government's exposure to AIG because, with the Treasury exchanging most of its preferred equity for common equity in January 2011 as part of AIG's recapitalization, our main focus is on the government's prospects for full recovery of the assistance provided and the progress and timing of that recovery thus far. The new indicators show (1) the progress in recovering the federal assistance through March 22, 2012, highlighting the amount of assistance drawn and recovered, the remaining assistance yet to be recovered, and the value of assets to be monetized to recover the remaining assistance; (2) the composition of the Maiden Lane II [this special purpose vehicle (SPV) has been fully liquidated] and Maiden Lane III portfolios; (3) the percentage distribution of the assets in those portfolios; (4) the distribution of the shares of AIG common stock outstanding that illustrates the government's level of ownership and equity exposure to AIG; and (5) one estimate of how long it might take Treasury to sell its common stock in AIG on the open market to help illustrate why we find that it would be more likely and practical for Treasury to sell its AIG stock to institutions.

To assess AIG's financial condition, we updated indicators of AIG's cash flows and its credit default swap (CDS) premiums and key credit ratings. To assess the financial condition of AIG's insurance companies, we compared the underwriting ratios for AIG with those of several of its peers. We have excluded the indicator on AIG's shareholders' equity that in 2008 was at risk of full depletion by massive losses if not for government assistance because AIG no longer faces such depletion risk and also is not at risk of such depletion while in the process of repaying the assistance provided. For example, AIG will not be required to buy back its common shares from Treasury to repay the assistance that was converted to common equity. Such a requirement would reduce AIG's equity. Instead, Treasury may recover much of that assistance by selling those shares to the public.[5] We excluded the indicator that tracks quarterly life insurance contract deposits and withdrawals because of dispositions that considerably reduced the size of this segment and because of the relative stability of the remaining businesses since 2009. Instead, our cash flow indicator tracks AIG overall cash flows that include the cash flow impact of this segment. We excluded the indicator on quarterly premiums written because AIG's business volume has remained fairly stable in 2010 and 2011. We also no longer update or include indicators that monitor AIG's progress in unwinding AIG Financial Products Corp. (AIGFP) because, as we discuss later, the company has reported that AIGFP's derivatives portfolio was largely wound-down as of the second quarter of 2011.

The data used to construct the indicators in this report came largely from AIG's public filings, Treasury, and the Federal Reserve. We have reviewed these data and found them to be sufficiently reliable for our purposes. We also used data from SNL Financial, Thomson Reuters, and Yahoo.com. We have relied on SNL Financial and Thomson Reuters data

---

[5]On March 13, 2012, Treasury sold 206,896,552 shares of its AIG stock at $29 per share. As part of this sale, AIG purchased 103,448,276 of those shares for $3 billion. This transaction is expected to reduce total AIG shareholders' equity by approximately $3 billion.

for past reports, and we determined that these data were sufficiently reliable for the purpose of presenting and analyzing trends in financial markets. Our reports also have relied on data from Yahoo.com, and in our review of these data we found them to be reliable for our purposes. We also reported data from four rating agencies. Although we have reported on actions needed to improve the oversight of rating agencies, we used these data because the ratings are used by AIG, Treasury, and market participants. We also relied on AIG's financial data, which we found reliable for our purposes.

We conducted this performance audit from February 2012 to May 2012 in accordance with generally accepted government auditing standards. Those standards require that we plan and perform the audit to obtain sufficient, appropriate evidence to provide a reasonable basis for our findings and conclusions based on our audit objectives. We believe that the evidence obtained provides a reasonable basis for our findings and conclusions based on our audit objectives.

Background

AIG is an international insurance organization serving customers in more than 130 countries. As of December 31, 2011, AIG had assets of $555.8 billion and revenues of $64.2 billion for the preceding year. AIG companies serve commercial, institutional, and individual customers through worldwide property/casualty networks. In addition, AIG companies provide life insurance and retirement services in the United States.

AIG Operations

AIG provides insurance and retirement services through several companies. More than 90 percent of the company's revenues in 2011 came through Chartis and SunAmerica Financial Group. Chartis offers property/casualty insurance and other products and services both in the United States and around the world commercially and to individual consumers, while SunAmerica Financial Group offers life insurance and retirement services. In 2011, AIG also generated 7 percent of its revenues in aircraft leasing operations. The remaining revenues were generated by its other businesses, which included among others, the remaining derivatives portfolio of AIGFP. According to AIG's 10K for 2011, the active wind-down of the AIGFP derivatives portfolio was completed by the end of the second quarter of 2011, and the remaining AIGFP derivatives portfolio consists predominantly of transactions AIG believes are of low complexity and low risk and support AIG's risk management objectives or are not economically appropriate to unwind based on a cost-versus-benefit analysis.

Federal, state, and international authorities regulate AIG and its subsidiaries. Until March 2010, the Office of Thrift Supervision was the consolidated supervisor of AIG, which was a thrift holding company by virtue of its ownership of the AIG Federal Savings Bank.[6] AIG has recently stated that it believes the company will be subject to additional regulation because of reforms contained in the Dodd-Frank Wall Street Reform and Consumer Protection Act to the extent that the statute and the regulations under it will affect the financial services they provide customers. AIG's domestic, life, and property/casualty insurance companies are regulated by the state insurance regulators in states in which these companies are domiciled.[7] These state agencies regulate the financial solvency and market conduct of these companies, and they have the authority to approve or disapprove certain transactions between an insurance company and its parent or its parent's subsidiaries. These agencies also coordinate the monitoring of companies' insurance lines among multiple state insurance regulators. Finally, AIG's general insurance business and life insurance business that are conducted in foreign countries are regulated by the supervisors in those jurisdictions to varying degrees.

In addition, Treasury's purchase, management, and sale of assets under TARP, including those associated with AIG, are subject to oversight by the Special Inspector General for TARP (SIGTARP). As part of its quarterly reports to Congress, SIGTARP has provided information on federal assistance and the restructuring of the federal assistance

---

[6]In 1999, AIG became a savings and loan holding company when the Office of Thrift Supervision granted AIG approval to organize AIG Federal Savings Bank. Until March 2010, AIG was subject to Office of Thrift Supervision regulation, examination, supervision, and reporting requirements. As the consolidated supervisor, the Office of Thrift Supervision was charged with identifying systemic issues or weaknesses and ensuring compliance with regulations that govern permissible activities and transactions. For more information on the role of consolidated supervisors, see GAO, *Financial Market Regulation: Agencies Engaged in Consolidated Supervision Can Strengthen Performance Measurement and Collaboration*, GAO-07-154 (Washington, D.C.: Mar. 15, 2007). As we reported in GAO-11-716 in July 2011, AIG reported that it has been in discussions with the Autorité de Contrôle Prudentiel and the UK Financial Services Authority regarding the possibility of proposing another of AIG's existing regulators as its equivalent supervisor.

[7]The primary state insurance regulators include New York, Pennsylvania, and Texas.

provided to AIG, as well as information on the unwinding of AIGFP and the sale of certain AIG assets.[8] SIGTARP's reporting on AIG's activities also has included reports that focused on federal oversight of AIG compensation and efforts to limit AIG's payments to its counterparties.[9] The Congressional Oversight Panel, which helped provide oversight of TARP, also issued several reports that reviewed the government's actions precipitating its assistance to AIG and executive compensation and identified several of its concerns with the rescue of AIG.[10]

Federal Reserve and Treasury Provided Assistance to AIG

In September 2008, the Federal Reserve, FRBNY, and Treasury determined through analysis of information provided by AIG and insurance regulators, as well as publicly available information, that market events at the time could have caused AIG to fail, which would have threatened the stability of financial markets.[11] Consequently, the Federal Reserve and Treasury took steps to help ensure that AIG obtained sufficient funds to continue to meet its obligations and could complete an orderly sale of its operating assets and close its investment positions in its

[8]SIGTARP, *Quarterly Report to Congress* (Washington, D.C.: Jan. 26, 2012); *Quarterly Report to Congress* (Washington, D.C.: Jan. 26, 2011); *Quarterly Report to Congress* (Washington, D.C.: Oct. 26, 2010); *Quarterly Report to Congress* (Washington, D.C.: July 21, 2010); *Quarterly Report to Congress* (Washington, D.C.: Apr. 20, 2010); *Quarterly Report to Congress* (Washington, D.C.: Jan. 30, 2010); *Quarterly Report to Congress* (Washington, D.C.: Oct. 21, 2009); *Quarterly Report to Congress* (Washington, D.C.: July 21, 2009); *Quarterly Report to Congress* (Apr. 21, 2009); and *Initial Report to the Congress* (Washington, D.C.: Feb. 6, 2009).

[9]SIGTARP, *Extent of Federal Agencies' Oversight of AIG Compensation Varied, and Important Challenges Remain* (Washington, D.C.: Oct. 14, 2009), and *Factors Affecting Efforts to Limit Payments to AIG Counterparties* (Washington, D.C.: Nov. 17, 2009).

[10]Congressional Oversight Panel, *June Oversight Report: The AIG Rescue, Its Impact on Markets, and the Government's Exit Strategy* (Washington, D.C: June 10, 2010); *February Oversight Report: Executive Compensation Restrictions in the Troubled Asset Relief Program* (Washington, D.C.: Feb. 10, 2011); and *March Oversight Report: The Final Report of the Congressional Oversight Panel* (Washington, D.C.: Mar. 16, 2011). Pursuant to EESA's requirements, the Congressional Oversight Panel terminated on April 3, 2011.

[11]In our March 2009 testimony on CDS, we noted that no single definition for systemic risk exists. Traditionally, systemic risk was viewed as the risk that the failure of one large institution would cause other institutions to fail. This micro-level definition is one way to think about systemic risk. Recent events have illustrated a more macro-level definition: the risk that an event could broadly affect the financial system rather than just one or a few institutions. See GAO, *Systemic Risk: Regulatory Oversight and Recent Initiatives to Address Risk Posed by Credit Default Swaps*, GAO-09-397T (Washington, D.C.: Mar. 5, 2009).

GAO-12-574 TARP: AIG Equity Investments

securities lending program and AIGFP. The federal government first provided assistance to AIG in September 2008 and subsequently modified and amended that assistance.

AIG's Financial Problems Mounted Rapidly in 2008

From July through early September 2008, AIG faced increasing liquidity pressure following a downgrade in its credit ratings in May 2008 due in part to residential mortgage-backed securities (RMBS) assets purchased with the cash collateral for the company's securities lending, which declined in value and became less liquid. In addition, the values of the collateralized debt obligations (CDO) against which AIGFP had written CDS protection declined in value, triggering collateral calls.[12] AIG attempted to raise additional capital in the private market in September 2008 but was unsuccessful. On September 15, 2008, the rating agencies downgraded AIG's debt rating, which further increased financial pressures on the company. Also around this time, the insurance regulators decided they would no longer allow AIG's insurance subsidiaries to lend funds to the parent company under an AIG revolving credit facility, and they demanded that any outstanding loans be repaid and the facility be terminated.

Concerns about an AIG Failure Led the Federal Reserve and Treasury to Assist AIG and Subsequently Restructure That Assistance

Federal Reserve's assistance to AIG. In September 2008, prior to TARP, AIG received government assistance in the form of a loan from FRBNY. In exchange, AIG provided shares of preferred stock to the AIG Credit Facility Trust created by FRBNY. This trust received 100,000 shares of Series C preferred stock, and Treasury received a 79.8 percent voting interest in AIG in exchange for FRBNY providing AIG a revolving loan.[13] On October 6, 2008, the Federal Reserve authorized the creation of the AIG securities borrowing facility (SBF) to provide up to $37.8 billion of direct funding support to a securities lending program operated by certain AIG domestic insurance companies. From October 8, 2008, through December 11, 2008, FRBNY provided cash loans to certain AIG domestic life insurance companies, collateralized by investment-grade debt obligations. AIG's borrowing under the AIG SBF peaked at $20.6 billion before the AIG SBF was fully repaid in connection with the creation

---

[12]CDOs are structured securities issued in tranches and backed by a pool of bonds, loans, or other assets.

[13]These preferred shares were later converted to common stock and transferred to Treasury.

of Maiden Lane II LLC in December 2008.[14] To provide further relief, in late 2008, FRBNY created two SPVs—Maiden Lane II LLC and Maiden Lane III LLC—to purchase some of AIG's more troubled assets.

- Maiden Lane II replaced the AIG SBF and was created to serve as a longer-term solution to AIG's security lending program liquidity problems by purchasing RMBS assets from AIG's U.S. securities lending portfolio, which were the source of significant demands on AIG's working capital. The Federal Reserve authorized FRBNY to lend up to $22.5 billion to Maiden Lane II, and in December 2008 FRBNY loaned the SPV $19.5 billion to fund its portion of the purchase price.[15] The facility purchased $39.3 billion in face value of the RMBS directly from AIG domestic life insurance companies.

- Maiden Lane III was created to purchase multisector CDOs on which AIGFP had written CDS contracts.[16] In connection with the purchase of the CDOs, AIG's CDS counterparties agreed to terminate the CDS contracts.[17] The Federal Reserve authorized FRBNY to lend up to $30 billion to Maiden Lane III, and in November and December 2008 FRBNY loaned the SPV $24.3 billion.[18]

In March 2009, the government restructured its assistance to AIG, which included reducing the debt AIG owed on the revolving credit facility by $25 billion. In exchange, FRBNY received preferred equity interests totaling $25 billion in two SPVs created by AIG to hold the outstanding common stock of two life insurance company subsidiaries—American Life

---

[14]The interest rate on AIG SBF loans was 100 basis points plus the average overnight repurchase agreement rate offered by dealers for the relevant collateral type.

[15]AIG also acquired a subordinated $1 billion interest in the facility to absorb the first $1 billion of any losses.

[16]A multisector CDO is a CDO backed by a combination of corporate bonds, loans, asset-backed securities, or mortgage-backed securities.

[17]AIGFP sold CDS on multisector CDOs. As a result, to unwind these contracts, Maiden Lane III was created to purchase the CDOs from AIG's CDS counterparties. In exchange for purchasing the underlying assets, the counterparties agreed to terminate the CDS contracts, thereby eliminating the need for AIG to post additional collateral as the value of the CDOs fell.

[18]AIG also paid $5 billion for an equity interest in Maiden Lane III and agreed to absorb the first $5 billion of any losses.

Insurance Company (ALICO) and AIA Group Limited (AIA). FRBNY's preferred interests were an undisclosed percentage of the fair market value of ALICO and AIA as determined by FRBNY.

Treasury's assistance to AIG. In addition to the FRBNY support, Treasury started providing TARP assistance to AIG in November 2008 by purchasing preferred shares (these were later converted to common stock). Using TARP funds, Treasury purchased $40 billion of Series D cumulative preferred stock, which was exchanged in April 2009 for $41.6 billion of Series E noncumulative preferred stock.[19] The difference of $1.6 billion was in accumulated but unpaid dividends on the Series D stock.[20] That same month, also using TARP funds, to strengthen AIG's capital levels and further reduce AIG's leverage, Treasury provided a $29.835 billion equity capital facility to AIG, whereby AIG issued to Treasury 300,000 shares of Series F fixed-rate noncumulative perpetual preferred stock and a warrant to purchase up to 3,000 shares of AIG common stock. As AIG drew on the facility, the aggregate liquidation preference of the Series F stock increased.

The January 2011 Recapitalization of AIG Changed the Composition of Federal Assistance

In January 2011, AIG, FRBNY, Treasury, the AIG Credit Facility Trust, AIA Aurora LLC (AIA special purpose vehicle—SPV), and ALICO Holdings LLC (ALICO SPV) implemented a plan to recapitalize AIG and restructure the government's assistance in a manner intended to facilitate the eventual sale of the government's AIG stock. First, using loans to AIG from the AIA and ALICO SPVs, AIG repaid FRBNY in cash all the amounts owed under the FRBNY revolving credit facility and FRBNY terminated the credit facility. Second, Treasury, AIG, and the AIG Credit Facility Trust took steps to exchange the various preferred interests in AIG for common stock.

---

[19]Cumulative preferred stock is a form of capital stock in which holders of preferred stock receive dividends before holders of common stock, and dividends that have been omitted in the past must be paid to preferred shareholders before common shareholders can receive dividends.

[20]Because the Series E preferred stock more closely resembled common stock, principally because its dividends were noncumulative, rating agencies viewed the stock more positively when rating AIG's financial condition.

- The trust exchanged its shares of AIG's Series C preferred stock for about 562.9 million shares of AIG common stock and subsequently transferred these shares to Treasury.

- Treasury exchanged its shares of AIG's Series E preferred stock for about 924.5 million shares of AIG common stock and its shares of AIG's Series F preferred stock for (1) preferred interests in the AIA and ALICO SPVs, (2) 20,000 shares of the Series G preferred stock, and (3) about 167.6 million shares of AIG common stock. AIG and Treasury amended and restated the Series F securities purchase agreement to provide for AIG to issue 20,000 shares of Series G preferred stock to Treasury.[21] AIG drew down the remaining available funds on the equity facility and used that amount to repurchase all of FRBNY's preferred interests in the AIA and ALICO SPVs. AIG then issued shares of common stock and transferred the shares and the repurchased preferred interests to Treasury in payment of the liquidation preference of the Series F preferred stock.

In addition, AIG issued to holders of AIG common stock, by means of a dividend, 10-year warrants to purchase up to 75 million shares of AIG common stock at an exercise price of $45 per share.[22] The AIG Credit Facility Trust, Treasury, and FRBNY did not receive any of these warrants. According to Treasury officials, the warrants were issued to address the AIG board of directors' desire to compensate existing shareholders for the dilutive effect of the recapitalization plan. Also, AIG used proceeds from the sale of ALICO and the initial public offering of AIA to reduce Treasury's preferred interests (aggregate liquidation preference) in the ALICO and AIA SPVs to approximately $20.3 billion.

---

[21]AIG drew down approximately $20.3 billion remaining under Treasury's equity capital facility tied to the Series F preferred stock. According to Treasury, $40 billion of Series E preferred stock was exchanged for AIG common stock, $20.3 billion of Series F preferred stock was exchanged for SPV preferred stock, $7.5 billion of Series F preferred stock was exchanged for AIG common stock, and $2 billion of Series F preferred stock was exchanged for Series G preferred stock. AIG designated the $2 billion in Series G preferred stock to be available after the closing for general corporate purposes under the Series G preferred stock. AIG's right to draw on the Series G preferred stock was made subject to terms and conditions substantially similar to those in the agreement. On May 27, 2011, the available amount of the Series G preferred stock was reduced to $0 as a result of AIG's primary offering of its common stock and the Series G preferred stock was cancelled.

[22]Exercise price is the price at which the option holder may buy or sell the underlying asset.

At the closing of the recapitalization, Treasury held approximately 1.655 billion shares of AIG common stock (at then-current stock prices, these shares were valued at about $49.148 billion), representing approximately 92 percent of the outstanding AIG common stock, and owned about $20.3 billion in preferred interests in AIA and ALICO SPVs. These investments gave Treasury an increased total exposure to AIG of over $69 billion.

As shown in table 1, as of March 22, 2012, approximately 1 year following AIG's 2011 recapitalization, Federal Reserve's and Treasury's exposure to AIG, excluding unpaid dividends and accrued interest, was $44 billion. Since AIG's recapitalization, most of the government's exposure has been in the form of Treasury's ownership of AIG common stock.

Table 1: Outstanding Government Efforts to Assist AIG and the Government's Remaining Exposure, as of March 22, 2012

Dollars in millions

Description of the federal assistance	Outstanding balance	Sources to repay the government
Federal Reserve		
FRBNY created an SPV—Maiden Lane II—to provide AIG liquidity by purchasing RMBS from AIG life insurance companies. FRBNY provided a loan to Maiden Lane II for the purchases. FRBNY also terminated its securities lending program with AIG, which had provided additional liquidity associated with AIG's securities lending program when it created Maiden Lane II.	$0[a]	Proceeds from asset sales, asset maturities, and interest were used to repay the FRBNY loan.
FRBNY created an SPV called Maiden Lane III to provide AIG liquidity by purchasing CDOs from AIGFP's counterparties in connection with the termination of CDS. FRBNY again provided a loan to the SPV to fund the purchases along with funds paid to the counterparties by AIG.	8,271[a]	Proceeds from asset sales, asset maturities, and interest will be used to repay the FRBNY loan.
Treasury		
The remaining preferred interests in the AIA SPV had an aggregate liquidation preference of approximately $16.9 billion following a partial repayment on January 14, 2011. From February through March 22, 2012, AIG used proceeds from various sales to fully repay the preferred interest on the AIA SPV, and certain participating returns attributable to the preferred interests.	0[b]	Proceeds from asset sales used to pay down the preferred interests.
Treasury received 1.655 billion shares of AIG common stock (approximately 92 percent of the company). On May 24, 2011, Treasury sold 200 million of these shares and on March 13, 2012, sold 206.9 million shares. These sales reduced Treasury's shares to 1,248.1 million shares (approximately 70 percent of the company).[c]	35,743[c]	Treasury's goal is to sell the shares over time to recoup taxpayers' funds.
Total outstanding assistance, excluding unpaid dividends and accrued interest	**$44,014**	

Sources: GAO analysis of AIG SEC filings, and Federal Reserve and Treasury data.

^aGovernment debt shown is the remaining principal owed for the Maiden Lane III facility as of March 22, 2012, and reflects principal only and does not include accrued interest of $718 million for the Maiden Lane III loan. On January 19, 2012, FRBNY announced that it sold Maiden Lane II assets with a current face value of $7.014 billion through a competitive process to Credit Suisse Securities (USA) LLC, and on February 8, 2012, it announced that it sold Maiden Lane II assets with a current face value of $6.2 billion through a competitive process to Goldman Sachs & Co. In March 2012, FRBNY sold the remaining securities in the Maiden Lane II portfolio and used proceeds to fully pay the remaining debt and accrued interest.

^bOn August 18, 2011, AIG reduced the remaining liquidation preference of preferred interests that Treasury holds in the AIA SPV to approximately $9.3 billion by applying the proceeds of $2.15 billion from the sale of Nan Shan Life Insurance Company, Ltd., its Taiwan-based life insurance company, to Ruen Chen Investment Holding Co., Ltd., for $2.16 billion in cash. Additional payments through November 1, 2011, further reduced the remaining liquidation preference in AIA SPV to approximately $9 billion. On March 22, 2012, Treasury announced that AIG fully repaid Treasury for its remaining preferred interest in the AIA SPV.

^cTreasury's cost basis in 1.655 billion AIG common shares of $47.543 billion comprises liquidation preferences of $40 billion for Series E preferred shares, plus $7.543 billion for Series F preferred shares. In addition, unpaid dividends and fees of $1.605 billion are to be repaid as part of the liquidation preference. On May 24, 2011, Treasury sold 200 million shares of its common stock in AIG, reducing its holdings from approximately 1.655 billion shares to 1.455 billion shares, and AIG sold 100 million newly issued shares of common stock, increasing the total number of outstanding common shares to approximately 1.9 billion. These transactions reduced Treasury's equity interest in AIG to approximately 77 percent. Treasury's overall cost basis in its remaining shares was $41.799 billion that was derived from its cost basis per share of $28.7269. Treasury's overall cost basis per share is the combined cost basis of AIG common shares within TARP ($43.53) and AIG common shares outside of TARP. Treasury received the common shares outside of TARP from a trust created by FRBNY for the benefit of the Treasury. The trust exchanged its AIG Series C preferred shares, for AIG common shares. The May 2011 sale included about 132 million AIG common shares within TARP on which Treasury had a realized loss and about 68 million AIG common shares, with no cost basis outside of TARP, on which Treasury had a realized gain. Overall, Treasury had a realized gain as the 200 million shares were sold at a higher price ($29 per share) than Treasury's overall cost basis. On March 13, 2012, Treasury sold 206,896,552 shares of AIG common stock at $29 per share, for total proceeds of $6 billion. This sale, plus Treasury's sale in May 2011, yielded total proceeds of $11.8 billion, including $7.79 billion from sales of AIG common stock within TARP. Remaining outstanding assistance to Treasury of $35.743 billion was computed by subtracting from $47.543 billion (Treasury's cost basis in 1.655 billion shares) proceeds totaling $11.8 billion from Treasury's sales of AIG stock in May 2011 and March 2012. The information does not reflect returns from the sale, announced by FRBNY on April 26, 2012, of some of the Maiden Lane III holdings through a competitive bid process to a consortium of financial institutions.

Federal Government's Exposure to AIG Continued to Decline in 2011; Further Reductions Depend on Future Market Conditions

As of March 22, 2012, the date Treasury announced that AIG had fully repaid Treasury for its remaining preferred interest in the AIA SPV, the government's exposure to AIG had decreased to approximately $44 billion.[23] We reported in July 2011 that this exposure had increased from $120.7 billion in September 2009 to $129.1 billion in December 2009 and then decreased to $86.1 billion as of March 31, 2011.[24] The reduction was due to several factors, including AIG's full repayment of the debt related to Maiden Lane II and the liquidation preference in the AIA SPV, as well as Treasury selling almost 407 million shares of the 1.655 billion shares AIG common stock it received in exchange for preferred shares in AIG as part of AIG's January 2011 recapitalization. We have developed three new indicators that show the composition and level of all government assistance to AIG at points in time, including the portfolio of assistance and AIG's repayment of that assistance as of March 22, 2012. Since AIG no longer has outstanding debt directly owed to the government and the government is focusing on recouping its common equity investments in AIG by selling its AIG stock and its remaining debt in Maiden Lane III by selling its investment portfolio, we have added new indicators to track these investments in greater detail. One of these new indicators tracks the level of Treasury's ownership of AIG stock.[25]

The Government Has Recouped Some of Its Assistance to AIG

Three new indicators track the changing composition and level of government assistance to AIG and where that assistance stood as of March 22, 2012. The first indicator shows the assistance available to AIG and the levels of assistance actually used since FRBNY provided its initial assistance to AIG in October 2008. Its purpose is to show the progress

---

[23]In table 1 we reported outstanding assistance to be $44 billion, which includes $35.7 billion in outstanding AIG common stock owned by Treasury—the portion of the original cost of the shares to be repaid. By contrast, figure 1 reports the remaining federal assistance to be $44.2 billion, which includes Treasury's $35.9 billion cost of its AIG common stock. This cost is the product of 1,248,141,210 shares multiplied by the original breakeven price of $28.7269 on all 1.655 billion shares AIG received as part of the recapitalization in January 2011 plus unpaid dividends.

[24]We reported the amounts for 2009 and 2010 in GAO-11-46, GAO-10-475, and GAO-09-975 .

[25]This new indicator replaces a prior indicator of the composition of the government's direct assistance to AIG before and upon announcement and execution of the recapitalization agreement because other new indicators allow us to focus more directly on the government's exposure to AIG through its remaining debt and equity investments.

AIG has made in repaying its assistance and changes in composition and level of that assistance.

This indicator (see fig. 1) covers both the debt and equity assistance from both FRBNY and Treasury. It shows that the maximum federal assistance available to AIG grew from $122.8 billion as of October 29, 2008, to $172.4 billion as of December 31, 2009.[26] Over the same period, the government's exposure fluctuated between 68 percent and 81 percent of this cap. The assistance included (1) FRBNY's loans through the revolving credit and secured borrowing facilities (the latter facility was opened for 2 months in 2008); (2) loans to Maiden Lanes II and III; (3) FRBNY's receipt of preferred interests in two AIG SPVs, namely AIA Aurora LLC and ALICO Holdings LLC; and (4) Treasury's purchase of AIG's Series D/E preferred stock and Series F preferred stock. By December 31, 2010, the assistance available to AIG had been reduced to $154.7 billion, primarily because of repayments from the Maiden Lane facilities. The amount of assistance both available and provided to the company was reduced as part of the January 2011 recapitalization that resulted in the government owning 92 percent of AIG's common stock. This ownership was reduced to approximately 77 percent in May 2011 after Treasury sold 200 million shares of its common stock in AIG and reduced further to approximately 70 percent in March 2012 after Treasury sold 206,896,552 shares.[27] As of March 22, 2012, outstanding government assistance was $44.2 billion, of which $35.9 billion or about 81 percent was in the form of Treasury's remaining holdings in AIG common stock and $8.3 billion was in remaining principal owed on Maiden III.

---

[26]The peak amount of assistance available to AIG was $182.3 billion.

[27]On May 24, 2011, AIG sold 100 million shares of common stock, which were issued on May 27, 2011, increasing the total number of common shares outstanding to approximately 1.9 billion. On May 24, 2011, Treasury sold 200 million shares of its common stock in AIG, reducing its holdings to approximately 1.5 billion shares, or approximately 77 percent of the equity interest in AIG as of May 27, 2011. On March 13, 2012, AIG bought half of the approximately 207 million shares of AIG common stock that Treasury sold on that date, which reduced total outstanding AIG common shares to approximately 1.793 billion and Treasury's holdings to approximately 1.248 billion shares and common equity ownership to approximately 70 percent.

Figure 1: Changes in Composition and Level of Federal Assistance through March 22, 2012

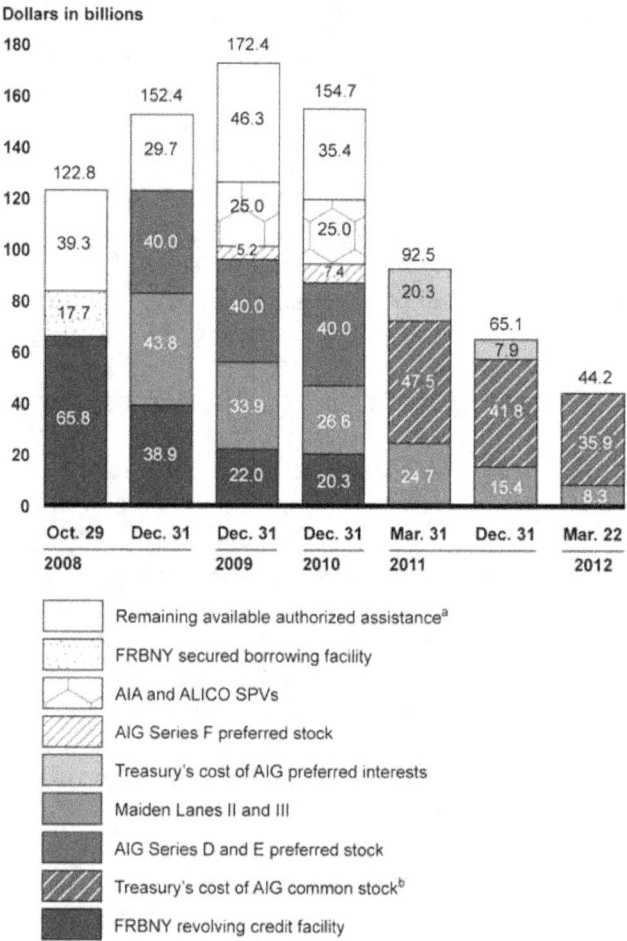

Dollars in billions

Source: GAO analysis of data from U.S. Treasury, Federal Reserve, and AIG and Yahoo.com stock price quotes.

Note: Amounts shown do not include accrued interest and dividends.

[a]Remaining available authorized assistance for October 2008 and December 31, 2008, was comprised of undrawn amounts on FRBNY's revolving credit facility, secured borrowing facility, and loans to Maiden Lanes II and III. For December 31, 2009, and December 31, 2010, this amount included undrawn amounts on Treasury's Series F facility.

[b]Treasury's cost of AIG Common Stock is the product of the remaining shares held by Treasury (1,655,037,962 shares on March 31, 2011; 1,455,037,962 shares on December 31, 2011; and 1,248,141,410 shares on March 22, 2012) times Treasury's original breakeven price of $28.7262 per share. Including unpaid dividends, the breakeven price would be $29.6967 per share.

To complement the previous indicator, we developed two indicators that provide more detail on the composition of the federal assistance. The first one lists each of the FRBNY facilities established to assist AIG,

Treasury's preferred equity interests in AIG, and Treasury's common stock in AIG, and the second shows the progress that AIG has made in repaying the federal assistance as of March 22, 2012. For each form of assistance the indicator provides (1) potential returns, (2) the total assistance drawn by or on behalf of AIG, (3) a summary of the debt that was restructured as preferred equity and the eventual exchange of the preferred equity for common equity, (4) accrued interest and dividend on all assistance provided, (5) the amount of the assistance that has been repaid and the amount that remains outstanding, and (6) the current value of the assets that are the sources to recoup or repay the remaining assistance. The purpose of the indicator is to summarize the activities of each form of assistance provided to or on behalf of AIG from the beginning in 2008 to the remaining assistance owed to the government as of March 22, 2012.

As shown in table 2, the FRBNY revolving credit facility has been repaid, including interest and fees, and closed. AIG's initial maximum authorized assistance (cap) under the facility was $85 billion. In November 2008, when Treasury repaid $40 billion of the assistance in exchange of Series D preferred shares, the facility's cap was reduced by $25 billion, which was $15 billion less than the $40 billion repayment. This effectively provided AIG access to $15 billion of additional assistance, which allowed it the opportunity to draw up to $100 billion ($15 billion plus $85 billion) on the credit facility. AIG's maximum draw on the facility reached $88.549 billion (including accrued interest), which occurred on April 26, 2010. The indicator also shows that for Maiden Lane II and Maiden Lane III, respectively, total assistance was $19.494 billion and $24.339 billion. As of March 22, 2012, the FRBNY loan and accrued interest on the Maiden Lane II facility were fully repaid. The remaining $8.989 billion in assistance owed (which includes accrued interest) all pertains to Maiden Lane III and the current value of assets to be monetized to pay back that remaining assistance is $17.449 billion. It also shows that a portion of Treasury's preferred equity interests (Series D/E and F) have been exchanged for AIG common stock. As of March 22, 2012, that assistance amounted to $37.3 billion (this includes $1.6 billion of dividends), which is to be repaid by the sale of AIG common stock, valued at $38.5 billion (1,248,141,410 shares of government-owned AIG stock at $30.83 a share, which was the closing price of AIG on March 30, 2012). Based on the composition of the remaining federal assistance to AIG, the repayment and recovery progress thus far on all assistance as of March 22, 2012, and the March 30, 2012, value of the remaining shares of AIG stock held by Treasury, the government could receive total returns of approximately $15.1 billion in excess of the assistance provided, including

Interest, dividends, and fees. This analysis does not include estimates of subsidy costs associated with the assistance.

Table 2: Composition and Repayment Progress of Federal Assistance to AIG, as of March 22, 2012

Dollars in millions

	Total	Revolving credit facility (RCF)[a]	Maiden Lanes II and III[b]	Series D/E	Series F	AIA and ALICO SPVs	AIG stock
Potential or realized return to the government in excess of assistance provided (interest, dividends, and fees plus net gain or loss)	$15,138	$6,700	$4,261	$0	$0	$1,440	$2,737
Total or maximum assistance drawn by or on behalf of AIG by facility[i]	$160,217	$88,549[a]	$43,833[c]	n/a[a]	$27,835[j]	n/a[a]	n/a
Debt restructured as preferred equity	0	(65,000)[a]	n/a	$40,000[a]	n/a	$25,000[a]	n/a
Preferred equity exchanged for common stock	0	n/a	n/a	(40,000)	(7,543)	n/a	$47,543
Interest, dividends, and fees on assistance provided	11,126	6,700	1,381[d]	n/a	n/a	1,440	1,605
Total assistance repaid by or on behalf of AIG	(125,006)	(30,249)	(36,225)	n/a	(20,292)	(26,440)	(11,800)[e]
Remaining assistance, including unpaid dividends and accrued interest, owed to the government	46,337	0	8,989[f]	0	0	0	37,348
Current value of assets to be monetized or pledged as security for repaying remaining assistance	55,929	n/a	17,449[f]	n/a	n/a	n/a	38,480[g]
Estimated gain or (loss) to the government on assistance to AIG	**$4,012**	**n/a**	**$2,880[f, h]**	**$0**	**$0**	**n/a**	**$1,132**
Potential or realized return to the government in excess of assistance provided							
• Interest, dividends, and fees	**$11,126**	$6,700	$1,381	n/a	n/a	$1,440	$1,605
• Estimated gain or (loss) to the government on assistance to AIG	4,012	n/a	2,880	$0	$0	n/a	1,132
Totals—return to the government	**$15,138**	**$6,700**	**$4,261**	**$0**	**$0**	**$1,440**	**$2,737**

Sources: GAO analysis of Treasury, Federal Reserve, and AIG data.

Note: N/a means not applicable.

[a]AIG's initial maximum authorized assistance (cap) under the RCF was $85 billion. In November 2008, when Treasury repaid $40 billion of the assistance in exchange of Series D preferred shares, the RCF cap was reduced by $25 billion, which was $15 billion less than the $40 billion repayment. This effectively provided AIG access to $15 billion of additional assistance which allowed AIG the opportunity to draw up to $100 billion ($15 billion plus $85 billion) on the RCF. AIG's maximum draw on the RCF reached $88.549 billion on April 26, 2010. On this date the $88.549 billion was comprised of $23.549 billion that AIG owed under the RCF, plus $40 billion of RCF borrowings previously repaid by Treasury in exchange for Series D preferred shares and $25 billion previously converted to preferred liquidation preferences in the AIA and ALICO SPVs.

GAO-12-574 TARP: AIG Equity Investments

[b]The values for the Maiden Lane facilities are as of March 22, 2012. For Maiden Lane II and Maiden Lane III, respectively, total assistance was $19.494 billion and $24.339 billion. As of March 22, 2012, the FRBNY loan and accrued interest on the Maiden Lane II facility were fully repaid. The remaining assistance owed all pertains to Maiden Lane III and consists of unpaid principal of $8.271 billion and unpaid interest of $718 million; current value of assets to be monetized to pay back remaining assistance was $17.449 billion.

[c]The Federal Reserve Board authorized the SBF that provided AIG access to $37.8 billion of direct funding support from October 8, 2008, through December 11, 2008, to a securities lending program operated by certain AIG domestic insurance companies. By providing overnight loans against investment grade debt obligations, the SBF was intended to reduce pressure on AIG's subsidiaries to meet demands for returning cash collateral by liquidating the portfolio of RMBS in strained markets. The interest rate on the SBF was 100 basis points—a common measure used in quoting yield on bills, notes, and bonds and represents 1/100 of a percent of yield—plus the average overnight repurchase agreement rate offered by dealers for the relevant collateral type. AIG's borrowing under the SBF peaked at $20.6 billion before it was fully repaid in connection with the creation of Maiden Lane II LLC. This $20.6 billion is included in the $43.833 of total borrowings on the Maiden Lane facilities.

[d]Interest income on loans totaling $1.381 billion consisted of accrued and paid interest of $80 million on the secured borrowing facility before it was closed into Maiden Lane II, $583 million paid on Maiden Lane II, and accrued and unpaid interest of $718 million on Maiden Lane III.

[e]On March 13, 2012, Treasury sold 206,896,552 shares of AIG common stock at $29 per share, for total proceeds of $6 billion. This sale plus Treasury's sale in May 2011 yielded total proceeds of $11.8 billion, including $7.79 billion from sales of AIG common stock within TARP.

[f]For Maiden Lane III, because the assets to be monetized have a greater fair value than the remaining assistance owed, the government is expected to be fully repaid. The information on Maiden Lane III does not reflect returns from the sale, announced by FRBNY on April 26, 2012, of some of the Maiden Lane III holdings through a competitive bid process to a consortium of financial institutions.

[g]This is the market value of 1,248,141,410 shares of government-owned AIG stock at $30.83 a share, which was the closing price of AIG on March 30, 2012.

[h]Total gain consisted of a $2.220 billion gain plus accrued interest of $580 million to FRBNY on the full repayment of the Maiden II loan and AIG's payment to FRBNY of $80 million for accrued interest on the secured borrowing facility.

[i]Each facility's maximum assistance drawn, when added together totaled $160.217. This amount is greater than the maximum assistance outstanding at any one time because the maximum amounts drawn occurred at different times for each facility. Specifically, on Dec 24, 2008, when the maximum amount drawn on the Maiden Lane facilities reached $43.833 billion, $80.018 billion was drawn on the RCF and Series F was not yet created; thus total outstanding assistance at that time was $123.851 billion. Around April 26, 2010, when the maximum amount drawn on the RCF reached $88.549 billion, only $7.543 was drawn on the Series F facility and $31.339 billion was owed on the Maiden Lane facilities, for total outstanding assistance of $127.431 billion. In January 2011, when the maximum amount drawn on the Series F facility reached $27.865 billion, the remaining balance still owed on the RCF was fully repaid and part of the $25 billion of preferred equity in AIA and ALICO was repaid as part of the recapitalization, while $26.303 billion was owed on the Maiden Lane facilities for total outstanding assistance of under $80 billion.

[j]As part of AIG restructuring that closed on January 14, 2011, $2 billion of authorized assistance under the Series F preferred shares was used to provide authorized assistance under Series G preferred shares. No amounts were ever drawn on the Series G facility and the authorized amount was reduced to zero when AIG issued common stock on May 27, 2011.

Figure 2 shows the progress that has been made in repaying the federal assistance to AIG as of March 22, 2012. As of that date, $125 billion had been repaid by or on behalf of AIG and the government had $46.337 billion in remaining assistance outstanding, including $11.1 billion in accrued interest and fees and unpaid dividends. The remaining assistance outstanding comprised $37.3 billion in AIG stock valued at $38.5 billion as of March 30, 2012, and $9 billion in debt and accrued interest owed to FRBNY by Maiden Lane III that is secured by assets valued at $17.4 billion as of March 22, 2012.

Figure 2: Repayment Progress of Federal Assistance to AIG, as of March 22, 2012

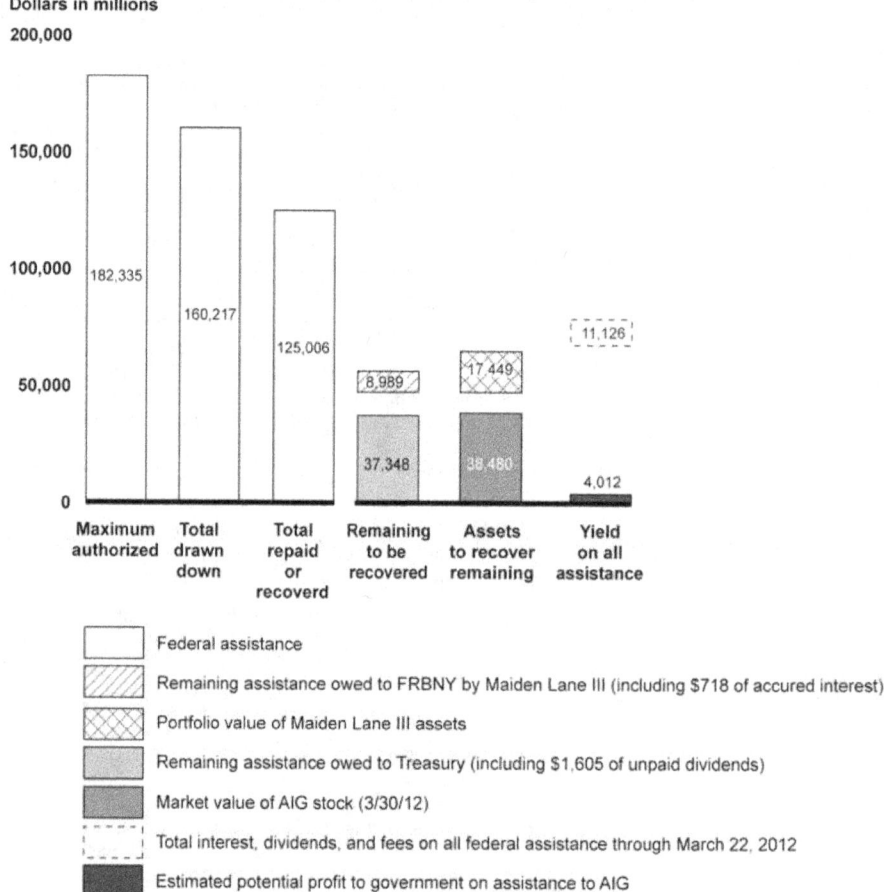

Dollars in millions

Federal assistance

Remaining assistance owed to FRBNY by Maiden Lane III (including $718 of accrued interest)

Portfolio value of Maiden Lane III assets

Remaining assistance owed to Treasury (including $1,605 of unpaid dividends)

Market value of AIG stock (3/30/12)

Total interest, dividends, and fees on all federal assistance through March 22, 2012

Estimated potential profit to government on assistance to AIG

Source: GAO analysis of AIG, Federal Reserve and Treasury data, and Yahoo.com stock price quotes.

Maiden Lane II Has Repaid FRBNY and Maiden Lane III's Assets Have Been Reduced Significantly

We also are monitoring the status of the government's indirect assistance to AIG through the Maiden Lane II and Maiden Lane III facilities. As discussed earlier, FRBNY provided loans to the facilities, giving Maiden Lane II capital to purchase RMBS from AIG's domestic life insurance companies and Maiden Lane III capital to purchase multisector CDOs from AIGFP's CDS counterparties. By monitoring the principal and interest owed on these facilities, we can track FRBNY's historical and ongoing exposure related to financial assistance it provided to AIG. The Maiden Lane II and Maiden Lane III portfolios were funded primarily by loans from FRBNY, which are not debt on AIG's books. At the time of implementation, the Federal Reserve had said that it planned to keep the Maiden Lane assets until they matured or increased in value to maximize the amount of money recovered through their sale but that it had the authority to change its portfolio strategy at any time. The loans and related expenses were to be repaid from cash generated by investment yields, maturing assets, and sales of assets in the facilities. Such cash was to be used to pay, in this order: operating expenses of the LLC, principal due to FRBNY, interest due to FRBNY, principal due to AIG, and interest due to AIG. Any remaining funds were to be shared between FRBNY and AIG, according to specific percentages for each LLC. In addition to the FRBNY investments in the facilities, AIG invested $1 billion in Maiden Lane II and $5 billion in Maiden Lane III. As of March 7, 2012, FRBNY had been fully repaid by Maiden Lane II, but the assistance to AIG through Maiden Lane III was not fully repaid. This assistance is the only debt owed to the government that relates to AIG and as of March 22, 2012, the principal and interest owed by Maiden Lane III had been reduced to $9 billion from $11.5 billion in July 2011.

Maiden Lane II has fully repaid FRBNY. As shown in figure 3, the portfolio value of Maiden Lane II, which was as high as $20 billion in December 2008, was reduced to $9.3 billion by the end of 2011. This occurred primarily because of cash flows from the facility's assets and in 2011 nearly $10 billion (face value) in assets were sold through auctions (see app. I). As of March 7, 2012, the facility had fully repaid the FRBNY loan, and as of March 21, 2012, the deferred payment or interest payable to subsidiaries of AIG had been reduced to zero and the SPV had net portfolio holdings of only $19 million.

To repay FRBNY, as we discussed in our July 2011 report, in early April 2011, FRBNY began offering securities in the Maiden Lane II RMBS portfolio for sale to a group of dealers on more or less a weekly basis through early June 2011, a strategy that it hoped would avoid market disruption.[28] FRBNY's investment manager, BlackRock Solutions, disposed of the Maiden Lane II securities through a competitive sales process. To maximize returns to the public, FRBNY did not stipulate a time frame for disposing of these assets. Through June 9, 2011, Maiden Lane II held several auctions and sold nearly $10 billion from its portfolio. As of March 7, 2012, the facility had fully repaid FRBNY the outstanding principal and interest.

---

[28]See GAO-11-716. Following an offer by AIG to repurchase the assets it had sold to Maiden Lane II, FRBNY announced on March 30, 2011, that it had declined AIG's offer. FRBNY and the Federal Reserve said this was done to serve the public interest of maximizing returns from any sale and promoting financial stability. In light of improved conditions in the RMBS market and a high level of interest, FRBNY stated that it would begin more extensive asset sales through a competitive sales process.

Figure 3: Amounts Owed and Portfolio Value of Maiden Lane II, December 24, 2008, through March 22, 2012

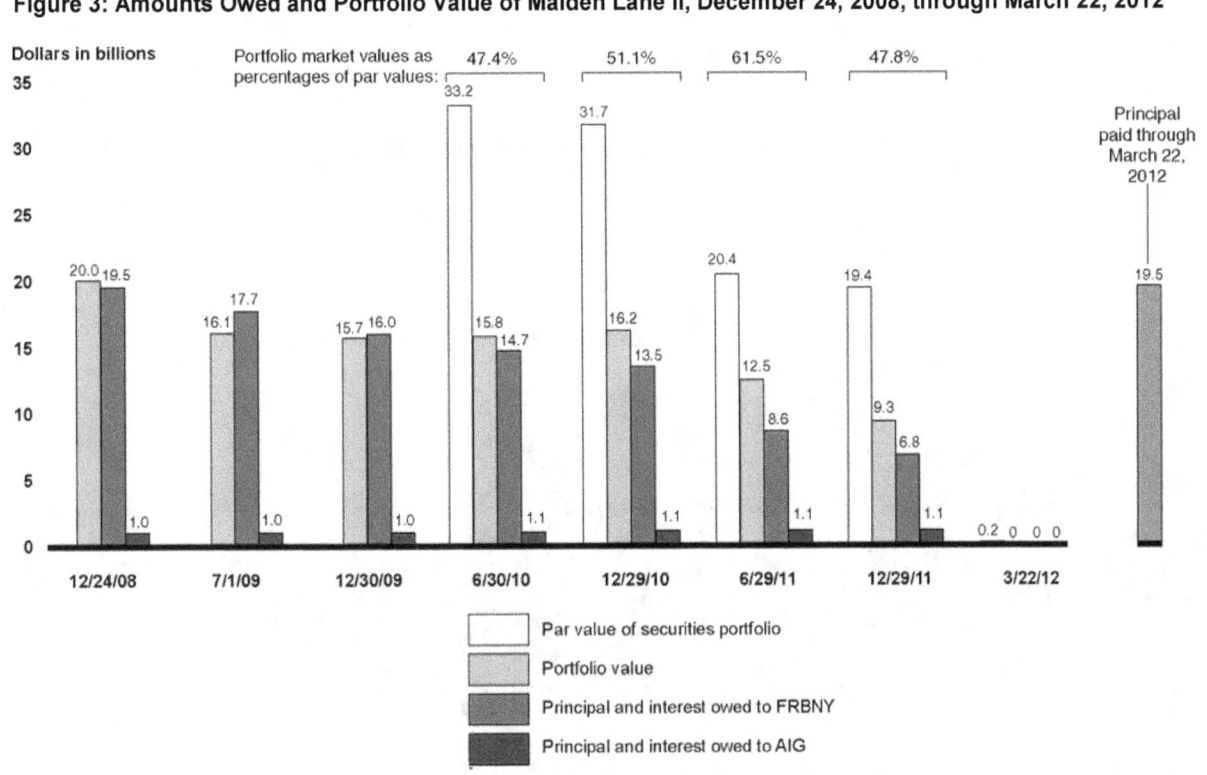

Source: GAO analysis of weekly Federal Reserve Statistical Release H.4.1.

Note: When Maiden Lane II was established in 2008, the par value of total securities purchased was $39.3 billion. Since January 2010, FRBNY has published the current principal balance for each security held by Maiden Lane II as of the end of the quarter.

As shown in the previous indicator, the outstanding loan balance was being reduced while value of the assets in the Maiden Lane II portfolio sometimes increased but mostly decreased by smaller amounts than the reductions in the outstanding loan balances; two new indicators show these assets in more detail.[29] The first indicator (fig. 4) is intended to show which categories of assets dominate the portfolio and which ones remain as the portfolio unwinds. The second indicator (table 3) shows the percentage distribution of the assets in the portfolio by category. Figure 4 and table 3 show that through December 2011, most of RMBS assets in the portfolio were subprime, followed by Alt-A adjustable-rate mortgages

---

[29]This is the most recent publicly available information as of April 1, 2012.

(ARM), "other", and option ARM. Figure 4 also shows that the portfolio experienced little change until the first auction of Maiden Lane II assets in April 2011 and then stabilized by June 9, 2011, the date of the last Spring asset auctions.

Figure 4: Portfolio Composition for Maiden Lane II, December 31, 2008, through December 31, 2011

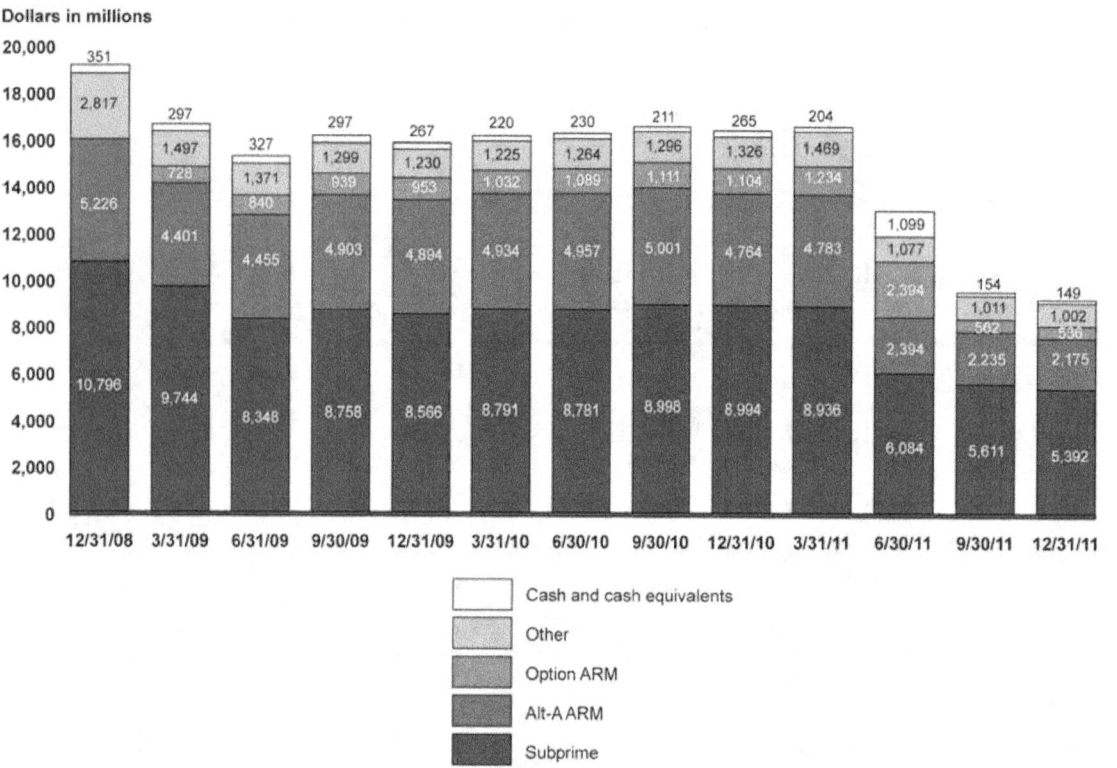

Source: GAO analysis of Federal Reserve data.

Note: In early April 2011, FRBNY began offering segments of the Maiden Lane II RMBS portfolio for sale to a group of dealers on a more or less weekly basis through early June 2011, a strategy that it hoped would avoid market disruption. Through June 9, 2011, Maiden Lane II held several auctions and sold nearly $10 billion from its portfolio. In addition, on January 19, 2012, FRBNY announced that it had sold assets with a current face value of $7 billion through a competitive process to Credit Suisse Securities (USA) LLC and on February 8, 2012, it announced that it sold assets with a current face value of $6.2 billion through a competitive process to Goldman Sachs & Co. More recently, on February 28, 2012, FRBNY announced the sale of the remaining securities in the Maiden Lane II portfolio, and as of March 7, 2012, the facility had repaid FRBNY the outstanding principal and interest.

Table 3 shows that the Maiden Lane II asset auctions generally resulted in transactions that minimally changed the distribution of the assets in the portfolio.[30]

Table 3: Percentage Distribution of the Assets in the Maiden Lane II Portfolio, December 31, 2008, through December 31, 2011

Securities sector	12/31/08	3/31/09	6/31/09	09/30/09	12/31/09	3/31/10	6/30/10	9/30/10	12/31/10	3/31/11	6/30/11	9/30/11	12/31/11
Subprime	57.3%	59.5%	55.6%	55.1%	54.8%	55.0%	54.6%	54.8%	55.6%	54.4%	59.8%	59.6%	59.2%
Alt-A ARM	27.7	26.9	29.7	30.8	31.3	30.9	30.8	30.5	29.4	29.1	23.5	23.7	23.9
Option ARM	–	–	5.6	5.9	6.1	6.5	6.8	6.8	6.8	7.5	6.0	6.0	5.9
Other	15.0	13.6	9.1	8.2	7.9	7.7	7.9	7.9	8.2	8.9	10.6	10.7	11.0

Source: GAO analysis of Federal Reserve data.

Note: Cash and cash equivalents are not included.

A second major round of auctions of Maiden Lane assets began in January 2012 and continued through late February 2012. According to FRBNY's February 28, 2012, announcement of its most recent and final securities sale from Maiden Lane II, all of the SPV's securities have been sold and the result is full repayment of the $19.5 billion FRBNY loan, plus $580 million in accrued interest on the loan and a net gain of approximately $2.8 billion. While the Maiden Lane II portfolio was still active, FRBNY officials noted Maiden Lane II's assets were high-quality bonds and thus they had expected to receive timely payments of interest and principal on most bonds in the portfolio regardless of the holding period. The assets continued to generate payments of interest and returns of principal at maturity while the portfolio was active.

Maiden Lane III continues to unwind. As shown in figure 5, the portfolio value of Maiden Lane III dropped from $28.2 billion in December 2008 to $22.7 billion 1 year later and rose slightly to $24.2 billion by June 29, 2011. From June through October 2011 the portfolio's value began to fall again but has remained fairly stable since then at just under $18 billion. During this period, principal and interest owed to FRBNY continued to be reduced from $24.4 billion in December 2008 to $9 billion (which included accrued interest of $718 million) as of March 22, 2012. Also, as of December 30, 2009, the excess in value of the remaining portfolio over

---

[30]This is the most recent publicly available information as of April 1, 2012.

the remaining FRBNY debt was about $4.2 billion and as of March 22, 2012, it had increased to about $8.4 billion. Overall, $16.1 billion of the principal on the FRBNY loan had been repaid as of March 22, 2012.

Figure 5: Amounts Owed and Portfolio Value of Maiden Lane III, December 24, 2008, through March 22, 2012

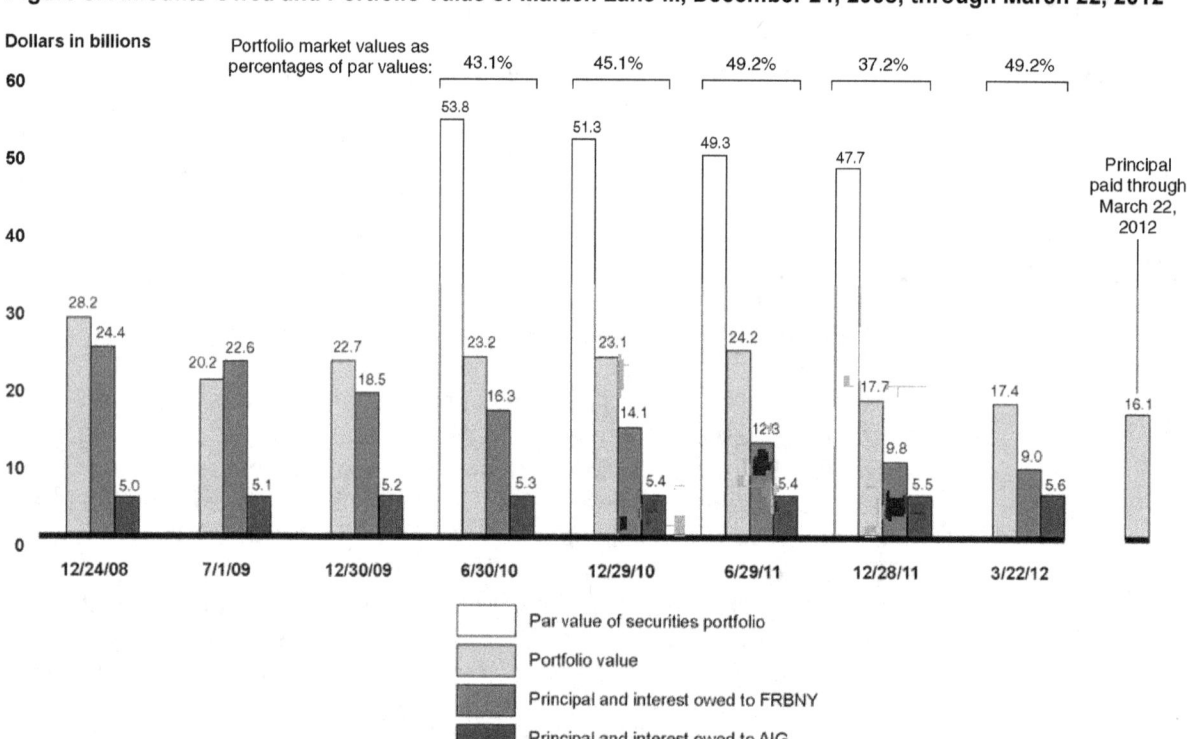

Source: GAO analysis of weekly Federal Reserve Statistical Release H.4.1.

Note: When Maiden Lane III was established in 2008, the par value of total securities purchased was $62.1 billion. Since January 2010, FRBNY has published the current principal balance for each security held by Maiden Lane III as of the end of the quarter. The information does not reflect returns from the sale, announced by FRBNY on April 26, 2012, of some of the Maiden Lane III holdings through a competitive bid process to a consortium of financial institutions.

As shown previously in figure 5 and as was the case for Maiden Lane II, the outstanding loan balance continued to be reduced while the value of the assets in the Maiden Lane III portfolio increased in some periods, but in some periods decreased, usually by a smaller amount than the reductions in the outstanding loan balances. We have developed two new indicators that show these assets in more detail. The first indicator (fig. 6) shows the extent to which certain assets make up the investment portfolio (to show which assets dominate the portfolio and which ones remain as the portfolio unwinds) and the second indicator (table 4) shows the percentage distribution of the assets in the portfolio. Figure 6 shows that through December 2011, most of the assets in the portfolio were high-grade ABS and commercial real estate CDOs.[31]

Figure 6: Portfolio Composition for Maiden Lane III, December 31, 2008, through December 31, 2011

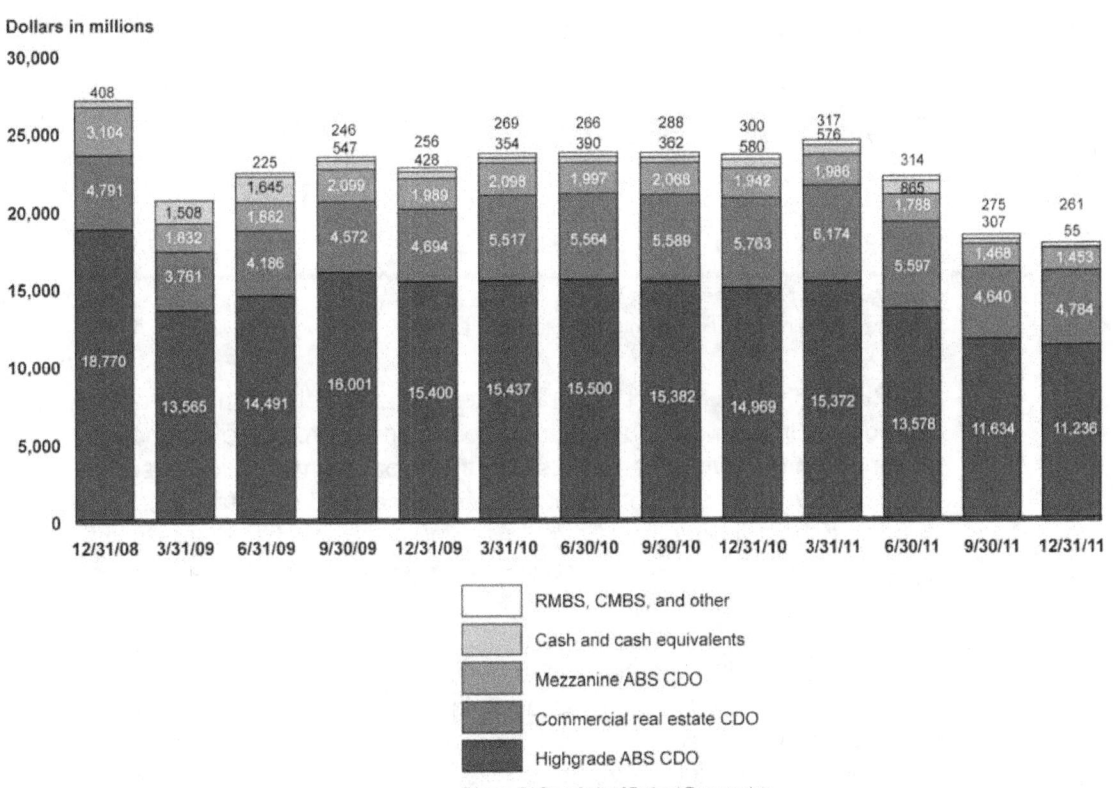

Source: GAO analysis of Federal Reserve data.

Table 4 shows that over the life of the facility, most of the assets have been high grade ABS CDOs followed by commercial real estate CDOs, while there have been relatively few RMBS, commercial mortgage-backed securities (CMBS), and other assets.[32]

---

[31]This is the most recent publicly available information as of April 1, 2012.

[32]This is the most recent publicly available information as of April 1, 2012.

Table 4: Percentage Distribution of the Assets in the Maiden Lane III Portfolio, December 31, 2008, through December 31, 2011

Securities sector	12/31/08	3/31/09	6/31/09	09/30/09	12/31/09	3/31/10	6/30/10	9/30/10	12/31/10	3/31/11	6/30/11	9/30/11	12/31/11
High grade ABS CDO	70.4%	70.8%	69.7%	69.8%	68.9%	66.2%	66.4%	65.9%	65.2%	64.5%	63.8%	64.6%	63.4%
Commercial real estate CDO	18.0	19.6	20.1	20.0	21.0	23.7	23.9	24.0	25.0	25.9	26.3	25.8	27.0
Mezzanine ABS CDO	11.6	9.6	9.1	9.2	8.9	9.0	8.6	8.9	8.5	8.3	8.4	8.1	8.2
RMBS, CMBS, and other	0.0	0.0	1.1	1.1	1.1	1.1	1.1	1.2	1.3	1.3	1.5	1.5	1.5

Source: GAO analysis of Federal Reserve data.

Note: Cash and cash equivalents are not included.

FRBNY officials expect to continue receiving timely payments of interest and principal on most bonds in the portfolio regardless of the holding period. In their view, the risk is that these payments could cease before the underlying portfolio has substantially matured or defaults could occur prior to the full repayment of outstanding principal.[33] The assets in the portfolio have continued to generate payments of interest and returns of principal at maturity.

Maiden Lane III's assets have continued to amortize and the long-term plan is for this SPV to sell the portfolio's assets to repay the debt. Federal Reserve officials said that they regularly evaluate opportunities to sell assets—while still meeting their objective of maximizing long-term cash flows—and have been able to sell a handful of assets across this

[33]Federal Reserve officials added that BlackRock Solutions, its investment manager for Maiden Lane III, currently produces moderate and extreme stress case scenarios to evaluate the potential risk to their outstanding loans if either significant downside shock were to occur. As of March 23, 2012, they said that BlackRock Solutions projected full repayment of interest and principal on the FRBNY loans to Maiden Lane III under the moderate and extreme stress scenarios. In early April 2012, the FRBNY changed the investment objective for Maiden Lane III, which now allows BlackRock Solutions to explore the sale of assets. There is no fixed timeframe for the sales; at each stage, the Federal Reserve will sell an asset only if the best available bid represents good value for the public, while taking appropriate care to avoid market disruption. On April 18, 2012, FRBNY announced that it has initiated a competitive bid process for the MAX CDO holdings in the Maiden Lane III portfolio.

portfolio. Their decision to sell an asset depends on an asset's discounted expected future cash flows and weighing those cash flows across scenarios by how likely they are to occur. Federal Reserve officials said that there has been no change in the approach to the disposition of Maiden Lane III assets.

All Assistance Associated with the ALICO and AIA SPVs Has Been Repaid

As stated earlier, the government restructured its assistance to AIG in March 2009. As part of that restructuring, FRBNY reduced the debt AIG owed on the revolving credit facility by $25 billion and in exchange, FRBNY received $25 billion of preferred equity interests in two SPVs created by AIG to hold the outstanding common stock of two life insurance company subsidiaries, ALICO and AIA. FRBNY's preferred interests were an undisclosed percentage of the fair market value of ALICO and AIA as determined by FRBNY. In November 2010, the company announced that it had sold ALICO to MetLife for approximately $16.2 billion (including approximately $7.2 billion in cash and the remainder in MetLife securities), and in October 2010 it announced that it had raised more than $20.5 billion in gross proceeds in the initial public offering of two-thirds of the shares of AIA. By January 14, 2011, the date of AIG's recapitalization, the aggregate liquidation preference of the AIA and ALICO SPVs had grown to approximately $26.4 billion. Following the sale of ALICO on January 14, a partial repayment by AIG reduced the aggregate liquidation preference of the remaining preferred interests to approximately $20.3 billion. These FRBNY preferred interests were purchased by AIG and transferred to Treasury (Treasury refers to these transferred amounts as "AIA preferred units" and "ALICO junior preferred units").[34]

Treasury received several repayments from AIG on its AIA and ALICO SPV investments in 2011 and 2012 that resulted in AIG fully repaying Treasury's remaining capitalization investment in both SPVs. In February 2011, AIG used $2.2 billion of proceeds from the sale of two life insurance companies to reduce the ALICO and AIA liquidation preferences, and on March 8, 2011, AIG used $6.9 billion from the sale of MetLife equity securities to repay Treasury's remaining $1.4 billion of preferred interests in the ALICO SPV and reduce by $5.5 billion Treasury's remaining

---

[34]Treasury exchanged its shares of AIG's Series F preferred stock for the preferred interests in the AIA and ALICO SPVs, along with 20,000 shares of the Series G preferred stock and about 167.6 million shares of AIG common stock.

preferred interests in the AIA SPV. Treasury received five additional payments throughout 2011 totaling $3.3 billion, and by November 2011, the remaining preferred interest on the AIA SPV had been reduced to $9 billion. Most recently, on March 22, 2012, Treasury announced that AIG had fully repaid Treasury for its remaining preferred interest in the AIA SPV.[35]

Treasury Would Have to Sell Its AIG Common Stock for at Least an Average Share Price of $29.70 to Fully Recover Its Assistance, Including Cash and Unpaid Dividends

The amount of the $37.348 billion (which includes unpaid dividends) in remaining equity assistance to AIG that Treasury will recoup depends on the prices at which it sells its remaining 1.248 billion shares.[36] As a shareholder, selling AIG stock with the goal of maximizing taxpayers' returns is a reasonable goal for Treasury. However, we have previously reported that as a government agency providing temporary emergency assistance, Treasury also is balancing this goal with exiting its assistance as soon as is practicable. Treasury has retained Greenhill & Co., LLC to advise it on selling and disposing of its AIG common shares. One way to measure potential return to the taxpayer is to track the performance of the company's stock price.

We have developed a new indicator that tracks total shares of AIG's common stock outstanding, including shares of that stock held by Treasury. The purpose of this indicator is to track the changing proportion of Treasury's remaining AIG common stock and the value of that stock as Treasury sells its remaining shares of AIG's stock to reduce its exposure to AIG.

Figure 7 shows that in December 2010, about 1 month before AIG's recapitalization, there were about 147.1 million shares of AIG common stock outstanding, most of which were held by Treasury. With the January 2011 recapitalization and the government exchanging its preferred shares for common shares, the number of AIG common shares outstanding was

---

[35]According to Treasury's announcement, Treasury had expected AIG to repay the remaining principal plus accrued interest and the AIA SPV with sales of ordinary shares in AIA and Maiden Lane II proceeds by mid-March 2012 and the release of escrowed proceeds from AIG's sale of ALICO to MetLife in two tranches, one by November 2012 and the remainder in May 2013.

[36]Treasury's cost basis in AIG common shares of $49.148 billion comprises liquidation preferences of $40 billion for Series E preferred shares, $7.543 billion for Series F preferred shares, and unpaid dividend and fees of $1.605 billion.

increased to 1.796 billion, with the government holding 1.655 billion, or about 92 percent, of the shares. Since the recapitalization, the government has reduced its shares and AIG has issued more stock. As we discussed in our July 2011 report, on May 24, 2011, a 300 million share offering to the public was priced, consisting of 200 million secondary shares from Treasury and 100 million primary shares from AIG. The transaction (all 300 million shares) closed on May 27, 2011, reducing Treasury's holdings to approximately 1.5 billion shares. On May 27, 2011, AIG issued and sold 100 million shares of common stock, increasing the total number of outstanding common shares to approximately 1.9 billion. As a result, Treasury held approximately 77 percent equity interest in AIG. As of December 30, 2011, the market value of Treasury's remaining shares in AIG was about $33.8 billion. Treasury's equity interest in AIG was reduced further to approximately 70 percent in March 2012 after Treasury sold approximately 207 million shares, half of which were purchased by AIG. When Treasury will sell its remaining AIG shares will depend on how future market conditions enable Treasury to meet its dual goals of maximizing taxpayer returns and exiting its exposure to AIG as soon as is practical.

Figure 7: Distribution of the Shares of AIG Common Stock Outstanding, the Market Value of Treasury's Share of AIG Common Stock, and the Percentage of the Stock Held by Treasury, September 2010 to March 2012

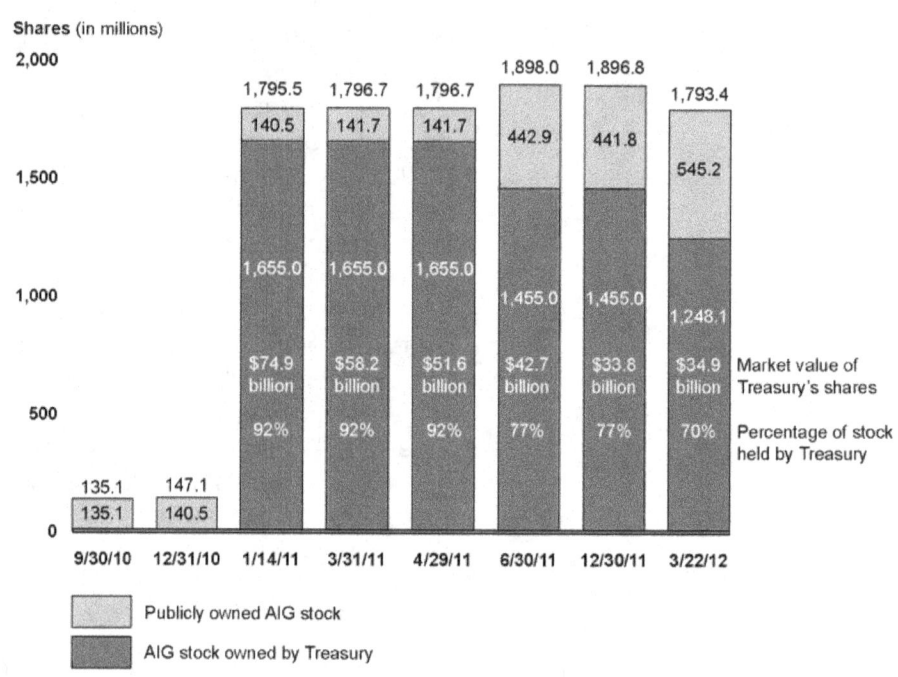

Sources: GAO analysis of AIG financial data and share price data.

Note: Total outstanding shares as of March 22, 2012, are reduced by 103,448,276 from the amount shown as of December 31, 2011, to reflect Treasury-owned shares that AIG bought on March 13, 2012.

The following indicator shows the market value of AIG's stock at various share prices and the profits or losses that Treasury would realize if it were to sell all of its stock at those share prices. A related indicator also compares month-end share prices of AIG common stock with Standard and Poor's (S&P) 500 index since the federal government began providing assistance to AIG in 2008. Treasury's cost basis of $49.148 billion for those shares was established as part of AIG's recapitalization plan, which was announced on September 30, 2010, and executed on January 14, 2011, when Treasury received 1.655 billion shares of AIG common stock to be the repayment source for the $49.148 billion. This cost basis comprises $47.543 billion of liquidation preferences in Series E and Series F preferred shares plus $1.605 billion of unpaid dividends and fees. Treasury said that its primary goal is to recoup taxpayers' actual cash outlays. As such, using the cash in/cash out approach, Treasury included only the cost of the liquidation preferences in the Series E and

GAO-12-574 TARP: AIG Equity Investments

Series F preferred shares—$47.543 billion—to calculate a breakeven share price to be $28.73. Under a different approach that captures the entire amount owed—$49.148 billion—the breakeven share price would include the $1.605 billion of unpaid dividends and fees and thus would increase to approximately $29.70. This amount represents the minimum average price at which Treasury would need to sell all of its shares to fully recover the $49.148 billion owed by AIG.

As shown in figure 8, the amount of the $49.148 billion Treasury will recover depends on the average price at which it sells its 1.655 billion shares of AIG common stock (the size of Treasury's holdings following AIG's recapitalization). The figure shows several share prices, some higher and some lower than the breakeven share price, to indicate how much of the full amount of assistance Treasury would recover at each price. For example, at an average price of $40 a share Treasury would recover an additional $17.1 billion, while at an average price of $25 a share Treasury would recover $7.8 billion less than the amount of assistance.

Figure 8: Market Value of AIG Common Stock at Various Average Share Prices

Average share price	At $20	At $25	Breakeven share price, including unpaid dividend At $29.6967	At $30	At $35	At $40	At $50	Breakeven share price, including unpaid dividend At $28.7269
Total value of market cap of AiG common stock	$35,909	$44,887	$53,319	$53,864	$62,841	$71,819	$89,773	$51,579
Value of 140.463 million publicly traded shares at particular average share prices	2,809	3,512	4,171	4,214	4,916	5,619	7,023	4,036

Dollars in millions except common stock share prices

	At $20	At $25	At $29.6967	At $30	At $35	At $40	At $50	At $28.7269
(Profit/Loss)	16,048	7,773	0	502	8,777	17,052	33,602	0
Series E + F	47,543	47,543	47,543	47,543	47,543	47,543	47,543	47,543
Unpaid dividends	1,605	1,605	1,605	1,605	1,605	1,605	1,605	

Average share price

Legend:
- Treasury's cost (unpaid dividends and fees)
- Treasury's cost ($40,000 in series E shares plus $7,543 in series F shares)
- Profit to Treasury / Loss to Treasury — if 1,655 million shares are sold at particular average share prices

Source: GAO analysis of AIG financial and share price data.

Note: Treasury's cost per share of $29.6967 comprises $40 billion plus $7.543 billion on Series E and F preferred shares, respectively, plus $1.605 billion of unpaid dividends and fees on Series D preferred shares.

From January 2011, when AIG was recapitalized, the daily closing share price of AIG stock trended downward but remained above our $29.70 breakeven price until May 24, 2011, when it closed at $29.46 (see fig. 9). More specifically, the price trended down from $45.25 per share on January 14, 2011, to $28.28 per share on May 25, 2011—its lowest price since early March 2010. This 37.5 percent downtrend reduced the value of Treasury-owned shares by $28.1 billion. In contrast, the S&P 500 index increased over this same period. The AIG share price reached a low of just over $20 per share in November 2011. Since then, however, the price has risen to $30.83 per share as of March 30, 2012, which is above

Treasury's $28.73 breakeven price excluding the unpaid dividend and the $29.70 breakeven price including the unpaid dividend. The current upward trend in the price of AIG common stock suggests that conditions for Treasury to sell its AIG shares have improved since November 2011. Responding to these conditions, as previously stated, in early March 2012 Treasury sold 207 million shares of its AIG common stock for $6 billion.

Figure 9: Month-End Closing Share Prices of AIG Common Stock Compared to the S&P 500 Index and Breakeven Share Price for Treasury's Remaining 1,248 Million Shares, September 2008 through March 2012

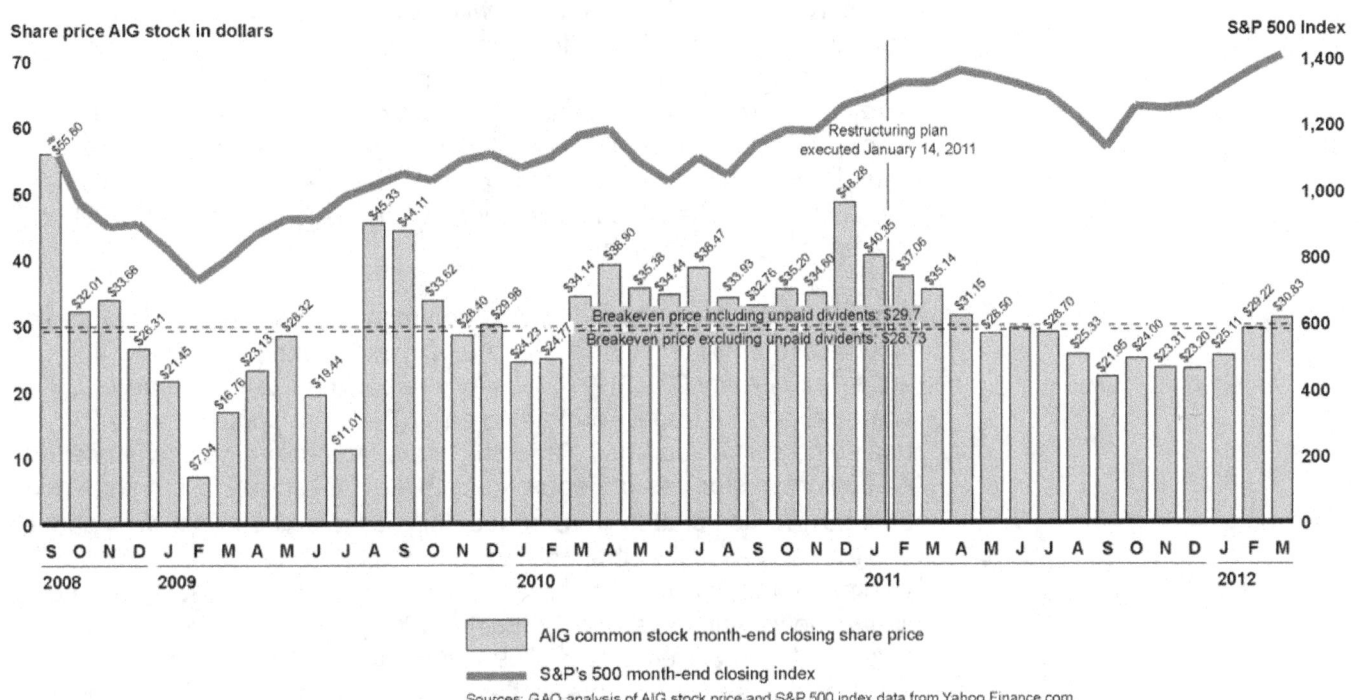

Sources: GAO analysis of AIG stock price and S&P 500 index data from Yahoo Finance.com.

Notes: AIG's share price was retroactively adjusted prior to July 2009 for the 1 for 20 reverse stock split that took effect on July 1, 2009. In January 2011, AIG issued 10-year warrants to AIG common shareholders as a 16.331455 percent dividend, as part of the Recapitalization Plan. None of the warrants were issued to Treasury or FRBNY. The warrants, which expire January 19, 2021, allow AIG shareholders of record on January 13, 2011, to purchase up to 74,997,778 shares of AIG Common Stock at an exercise price of $45 per share. AIG share prices prior to January 2011 (back to July 2009) are actual closing prices and not adjusted for this dividend.

Treasury Might Seek Large Institutional Buyers for Its AIG Stock

To better understand the options available to Treasury for selling its remaining AIG common stock, we have developed a set of indicators that examine the prospects of selling the stock on the open market versus selling it to institutional buyers. The first indicator shows how long it would take Treasury to sell its remaining shares of AIG common stock in the open market if it decided to pursue this approach. Following sales of 200 million shares in May 2011 and approximately 207 million shares in March 2012, Treasury's ownership of AIG common stock stood at 1.248 billion shares, or 70 percent, of AIG's common stock. These shares are to be sold to recoup the remaining $37.348 billion (including unpaid dividends) in equity assistance to AIG. The government's full recovery of this portion of assistance to AIG is tied to Treasury's prospects for selling AIG stock. Those prospects depend on the share price discussed earlier, investor interest, and the period over which Treasury sells its stock. Treasury officials told us that they will consider offers by institutions, sovereign funds, retail investors, and others. This indicator provides the number of trading days in a month and the number of months it would take to sell Treasury's remaining 1.248 billion shares of AIG common stock, based on average daily trading volumes over rolling 12 month periods. This metric is intended to provide perspective on the challenges Treasury would likely face if it intended to sell its remaining 1.248 billion shares in the open market.

Figure 10 shows that based on AIG common stock's average daily trading volume of 8.1 million shares over the 12 month period from March 1, 2011, to February 29, 2012, Treasury's remaining 1.248 billion AIG shares represent about 155 trading days (there are approximately 252 trading days in a year) or 7.4 months of average daily trading volume in AIG common stock as of February 29, 2012.[37] Over this 12 month period, about 8.1 million shares were traded daily, on average, which was about 1 million shares higher than the 7.1 million share average daily trading volume for the rolling 12 month period that ended March 31, 2011. The figure shows that if average 12 month trading volumes were to increase to levels that occurred in late 2009 and most of 2010, the remaining common shares would represent as little as 3 months of daily trading volume.

---

[37]We are using the most recent full month prior to the March 22, 2012, cut-off that we have been using for several of our other indicators.

Figure 10: Number of Trading Days and Months It Would Take to Sell 1,248 Million Shares of AIG Common Stock Using Average Daily Trading Volume Over Rolling 12 Month Period from the Fourth Quarter of 2008 Through February 29, 2012

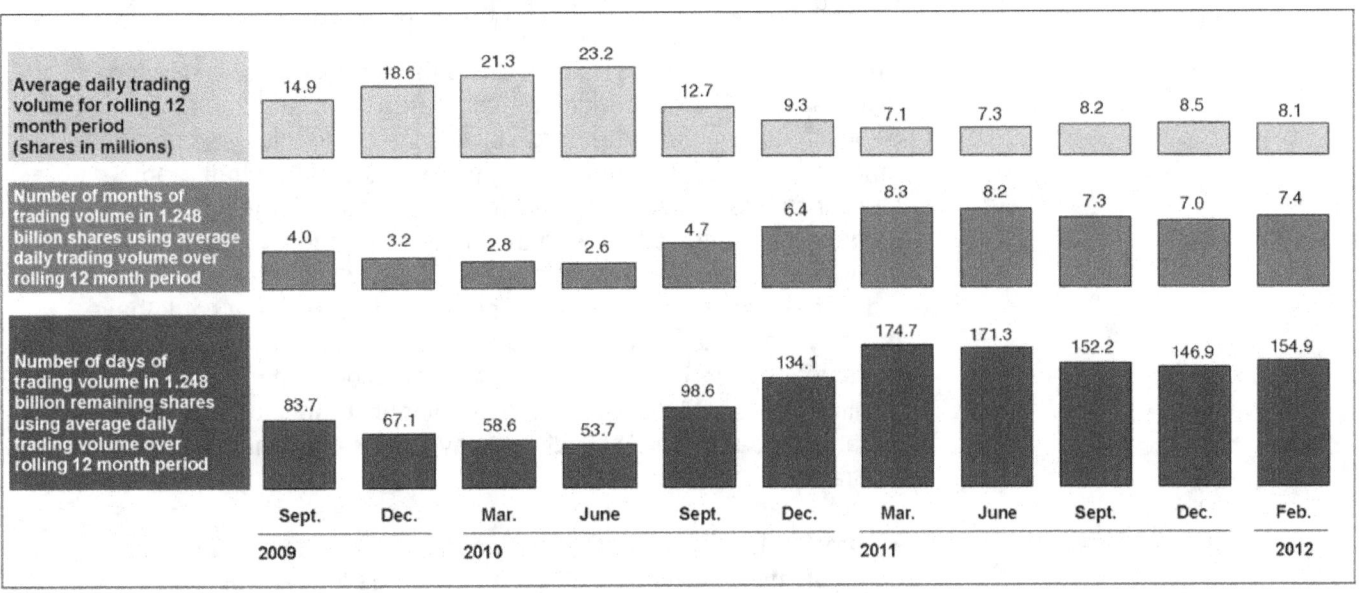

Source: GAO analysis of daily trading volume data from Yahoo Finance.com

Note: Calculations did not factor the potential for trading volume to increase with the increasing public float as shares held by Treasury are sold.

These measures of trading volume in days suggests how long it might take Treasury to sell its remaining AIG stock if it attempted to become a daily active seller in the open market. However, for the open market to accommodate such active selling by Treasury, at levels that match existing average trading volume without considerable downward pressure on AIG's stock price, existing and new buyers would have to collectively double the current daily buying volume. Whether such increased buying of AIG stock would enter the market to accommodate such selling by Treasury is unknown. Our analysis suggests that it would not be feasible to expect Treasury to be able to sell its remaining 1.248 billion shares of AIG stock in an orderly manner in the open market, which supports the agency's stated strategy of selling its stock in large blocks to institutional investors.[38] This strategy of selling to institutional investors also may help

[38]Institutional investors include mutual funds, pension funds, trust funds, foundations, endowments, investment banks, and other nonindividual organization investors that hold large volumes of securities and qualify for fewer investor protection regulations because they are assumed to be knowledgeable investors.

GAO-12-574 TARP: AIG Equity Investments

Treasury balance its competing goals of maximizing returns as a shareholder and exiting the investment as government agency as soon as practical.

The next two indicators help illustrate the prospects for institutional ownership of AIG. One indicator compares the market capitalization of AIG with that of nine other large insurance companies and compares the amount of stock the federal government holds in AIG to the amount of stock institutional investors hold in the nine other large insurance companies. Institutional ownership in the nine other large insurance companies could indicate potential institutional interest in AIG. While this indicator is helpful in demonstrating that AIG eventually could have majority institutional ownership like other large insurance companies, it does not capture the full potential for institutional interest in AIG because it is limited to institutional holdings in nine insurance companies. A second indicator more broadly portrays the institutional ownership of insurance companies.

Figure 11 shows that institutional investors collectively have majority common stock ownership of each of the nine large insurance companies. This finding is consistent with comments by Treasury officials that insurance companies tend to be largely held by institutional investors, which suggests that Treasury may look to institutional investors to purchase most of its AIG stock. The data, obtained for March 5, 2012, show that institutional investors own on average 82.6 percent of the companies. The ownership ranges from a low of 64 percent for Prudential Financial to a high of 99 percent for CNA. The market value of institutional holdings ranged from $7.7 billion (of CNA) to $30.2 billion (of MetLife). Thus institutional holdings in each of the nine insurers are smaller than Treasury's holdings in AIG of $44.2 billion. If institutions were to purchase the remaining AIG shares held by Treasury in proportion to their 82.6 percent average ownership in the nine companies, the amount would be $36.5 billion (which is 82.6 percent of $44.2 billion). This amount would be considerably larger than institutional ownership in each of the other nine institutions and raises questions about whether institutions collectively might desire or have the capacity to acquire $36.5 billion of AIG stock.

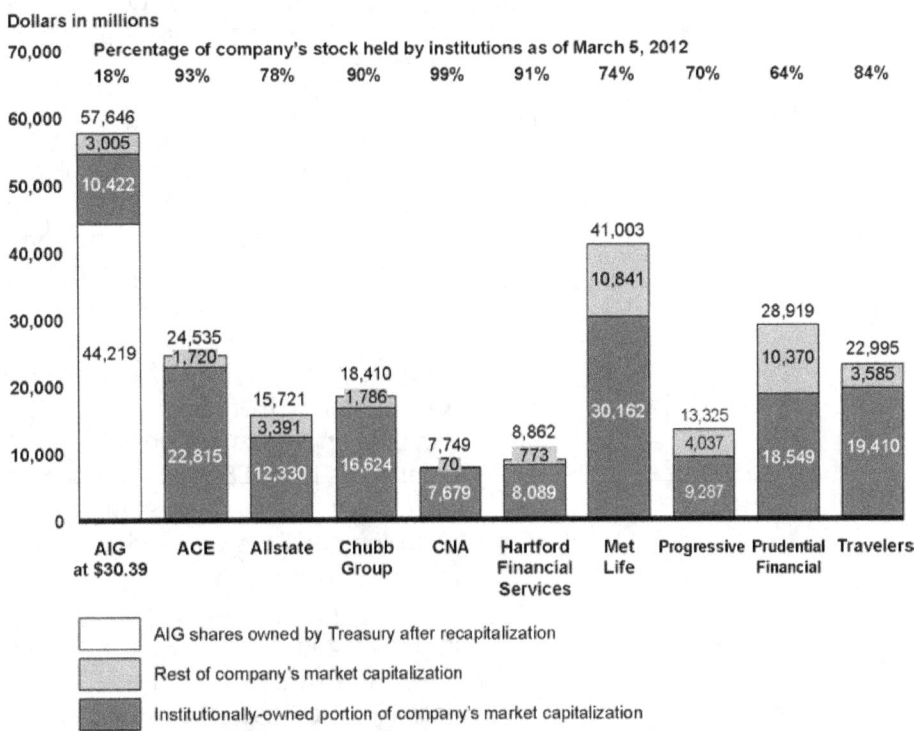

Figure 11: Market Values of Institutional and Other Holdings of Common Stock in AIG and Nine Other Insurers Based on Share Prices on March 5, 2012

Dollars in millions

Percentage of company's stock held by institutions as of March 5, 2012

| | 18% | 93% | 78% | 90% | 99% | 91% | 74% | 70% | 64% | 84% |

☐ AIG shares owned by Treasury after recapitalization

☐ Rest of company's market capitalization

■ Institutionally-owned portion of company's market capitalization

Sources: GAO analysis of market capitalization and percentages of institutional holdings data from SNL Financial.

Notes: We identified, but did not include in our analysis for this figure, 25 other insurers, each with a market capitalization larger than $8 billion as of March 8, 2011. The combined market capitalization of the 25 insurers was $866 billion. CNA is 89.99 percent owned by Loews Corp.

Institutions with the largest insurance holdings may consider adding AIG stock to their existing insurance holdings, and such institutions may have the greatest capacity to buy Treasury's AIG stock. To analyze whether institutions collectively might have the capacity to acquire most of Treasury's AIG stock, we developed an indicator on the aggregate insurance holdings of 1,979 institutions as of March 2012. This indicator is broader than that shown in figure 11 because it identifies and quantifies all insurance holdings of the 1,979 institutions. The premise behind the indicator is that institutions that have existing insurance holdings also might consider acquiring stock in AIG. The indicator provides the aggregate insurance holdings of the institutions that invest in AIG and nine other large insurers. As such, it may be useful for determining whether these institutions could have the capacity to purchase Treasury's AIG stock. The indicator is not intended as a device for speculating about whether the institutions should or will purchase AIG stock. Also, it is not known whether other institutions with considerable insurance holdings might exist that, if added to our analysis, would make total institutional insurance holdings considerably larger than aggregate amounts shown in the indicator.

Figure 12 shows that 1,979 institutions with existing insurance holdings may have the resources to consider buying Treasury's remaining stock in AIG. The figure shows that, using data from late April and early May 2011, the 1,979 institutions have an average of 14.2 percent of their holdings in insurance companies. Of these institutions, 1,392 each had insurance holdings of less than $100 million (totaling $26.5 billion), and 587 each had insurance holdings of more than $100 million. Among these institutions, as the size of an institution's insurance holdings increases, the percent of their holdings in insurance companies decreases. For example, investors with less than $100 million invested in insurance companies have 88 percent of their aggregate investments in these companies, but the largest two groups of investors—those with between $4 billion and $5 billion and those with more than $5 billion invested in insurance companies—have 13.1 percent and 6.3 percent, respectively, of their aggregate investments in insurance companies. Consequently, larger institutional investors might have a greater capacity to invest in Treasury's AIG stock. If the 19 institutions with the largest insurance portfolios increased their insurance holdings to the 14.2 percent aggregate average of these holdings for all 1,979 institutions, their insurance investments would increase by $300 billion, considerably larger than the $47.5 billion of AIG stock Treasury received as part of AIG's recapitalization. For these 19 institutions a percentage point increase in their insurance holdings would amount to $38 billion, as these institutions have combined total portfolio holdings of $3.8 trillion ($239.5 billion divided by 6.3 percent). Thus, $47.5 billion of AIG stock would raise their insurance holdings from 6.3 percent to 7.6 percent. This suggests that should they choose to do so, these institutions, as a group, have the capacity to purchase $47.5 billion of AIG stock without concentrating their holdings in insurance or considerably changing the distribution of their holdings by industry.

Figure 12: Approximate Number and Aggregate Market Values of Insurance Holdings for 1,979 Institutions, from Data Obtained in Late April and Early May 2011

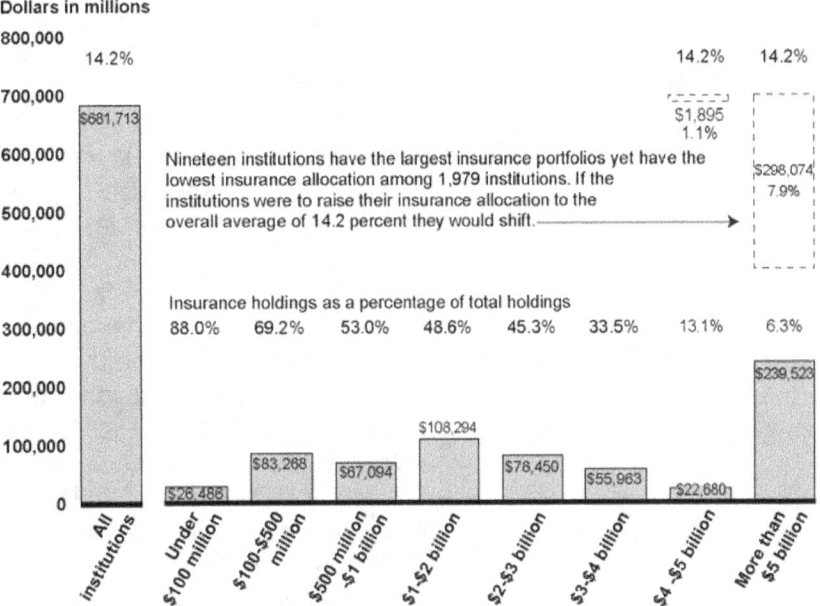

Dollars in millions

Nineteen institutions have the largest insurance portfolios yet have the lowest insurance allocation among 1,979 institutions. If the institutions were to raise their insurance allocation to the overall average of 14.2 percent they would shift. ────────→

Insurance holdings as a percentage of total holdings

| | 88.0% | 69.2% | 53.0% | 48.6% | 45.3% | 33.5% | 13.1% | 6.3% |

Institutions that each have insurance holdings of:

Number of institutions per holdings category

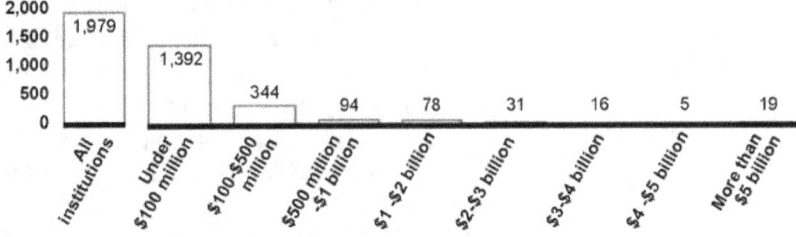

Institutions that each have insurance holdings of:

Source: GAO analysis of institutional insurance holdings data per SNL Financial.

Notes: The 1,979 institutions were identified as shareholders in the nine large insurers analyzed in figure 12. The nine insurers are ACE, Allstate, Chubb, CNA, Hartford Financial Services, MetLife, Progressive, Prudential Financial, and Travelers. Data on total insurance holdings of the 1,979 institutions were collected in late April and early May 2011. SNL Financial data on institutional stock holdings are from each institution's latest available quarterly Form 13F filing with SEC. The latest available quarterly Form 13F filings differed among the 1,979 institutions at the time of our analysis. SNL Financial daily updates the market values of these holdings using daily stock prices. Because of the volume of data used in this analysis, we could not obtain market values of holdings for all 1,979 institutions as of a single day. Rather, we used data over several days from late April to early May 2011. Thus, the aggregates for institutional holdings reflect quarterly 13F filings and market value dates that differ among the 1,979 institutions.

AIG's Financial Condition and Insurance Operations Have Remained Stable Since July 2011

With the government still holding the majority of AIG's common stock, a critical question is whether AIG's financial condition and operating performance and external perceptions about its financial condition and operating performance can remain strong enough for the government to recoup its investment. In 2011, two-thirds of the company's revenues were from its Chartis property/casualty and general insurance business and a quarter were from their Sun Financial life insurance and retirement services businesses. In 2011 the company also reported net income of $18.5 billion, which was up $8.5 billion from 2010 and continued the reversal of losses reported in 2009 and 2008. The $8.5 billion increase in net income was primarily attributable to the favorable effect of an income tax benefit in 2011 versus tax expense in 2010 partially offset by the absence in 2011 of gains recognized in 2010 on sales of properties and divested businesses. When gains and losses from sales of properties and divested business are excluded AIG showed a loss from continuing operations before taxes of $1.139 billion in 2011 versus a profit of $169 million in 2010. This reduction occurred because reduced operating expenses were not fully offset by reduced revenues from the absence of the full contribution of discontinued businesses. The indicators in this section show that AIG's financial condition and operating results have remained relatively stable. To track AIG's financial condition, we have indicators of AIG's cash flows, CDS premiums on AIG, and AIG's credit ratings.[39] The company maintained stable net cash flows from operating, investing, and financing activities throughout 2010 and 2011 while federal assistance was reduced including as part of AIG's recapitalization. The prices offered for CDS on AIG decreased and stabilized starting May 2009 and have remained fairly stable through March 2012. AIG's credit ratings also have remained stable since the first quarter of 2011. To assess the financial condition of AIG's insurance companies, we reviewed

---

[39]Since our previous update in July 2011, we have stopped tracking some indicators that we used to track AIG's financial condition. As noted previously, we no longer include the indicator on AIG's shareholders' equity which, in 2008, would have been fully depleted by massive losses, if not for government assistance. We no longer include it because AIG has maintained positive equity since the government assistance 2008 and no longer appears to face risk of depletion from losses. Also, AIG will not be required to repay assistance by buying back all AIG common shares now held by Treasury. Such a transaction could considerably reduce AIG's equity.

the underwriting profitability of these companies as a group.[40] We found that since the first quarter of 2010, the underwriting costs relative to premium revenues of AIG's property/casualty companies have been higher than peers on average, but that AIG's companies' net income was positive because of investment income.

AIG Maintained Stable Net Cash Flows While Reducing Federal Assistance to a Considerable Degree

AIG maintained stable cash flows throughout 2011 at levels much improved over 2008, although divestures of certain AIG businesses since 2007 have made AIG a smaller organization. During the first three quarters of 2007, AIG generated cash from its operating activities which indicated that it was profitable. It also generated cash through its financing activities, which indicated that it had access to the capital markets and used cash in its investing activities which indicated that it was growing its income-producing assets. The indicator of cash flows and net changes in cash tracks cash flows from operating, financing and investing activities and the combined net changes in cash from these activities. It uses data from AIG's quarterly and annual *Consolidated Statements of Cash Flows*.

- *Operating activity cash* flows indicate whether the company's core businesses are profitable.

- *Financing activity cash flows* indicate the extent to which a company uses the capital markets for equity and debt financing such as issuing its stock, bonds, and commercial paper to investors and obtaining bank loans and other forms of bank credit.

- *Investing activity cash flows* indicate the extent to which a company invests in its production capacity and efficiency (capital expenditures), acquires and divests businesses, and has financial investments such as stocks and bonds.

---

[40]We also have no longer include indicators that track the financial performance and condition of AIG's insurance companies. We no longer include the indicator on quarterly life insurance contract deposits and withdrawals because divestitures have considerably reduced the size of this segment and its impact on AIG overall and also because our cash flow indicator on AIG's overall operating, financing and investing cash flow captures the cash flow impact of insurance contract deposits. Also we excluded the indicator on quarterly dollar volume of insurance premiums written because AIG's premium volume over the past several quarters has remained fairly stable.

Generally, a healthy and growing company can generate cash internally from operations, generate cash externally from financing activities, and use this cash for growth in its operations or investments in income-yielding financial assets.

As shown in figure 13, AIG began to stabilize its cash flows in 2009 and maintained stable cash flows throughout 2010 and 2011. However, the composition of its cash flows in 2011 changed from that of 2009 and 2010. After reporting operating cash flows of $16.9 billion and $18.6 billion in 2010 and 2009, respectively, the company reported operating cash flows of $35 million in 2011, which was the lowest since the $755 million reported for 2008, as originally reported (this was restated as negative $122 million in its 2010 10K). The decline in operating cash flows in 2011 was mostly due to $6.4 billion of cash payments covering several years of accrued interest and fees on the FRBNY credit facility and a $10.4 billion reduction in cash flows from the absence of a full year of operating cash flows of foreign life subsidiaries (AIA, ALICO, AIG Star, AIG Edison, and Nan Shan) that were sold during the year. Payments on catastrophic loss claims and asbestos liabilities also reduced operating cash flows. Without these payments and reductions, operating cash flows in 2011 could have been at least $16.8 billion. However, AIG's net change in cash from all cash flow activities combined in 2011 did not change considerably from that reported in 2010 and 2009 as net cash used in financing activities was largely offset by net cash generated from investing activities. Net cash used in financing activities was higher in 2011 primarily due to full repayment of the FRBNY credit facility and partial repayment of the SPV preferred interests in connection with the recapitalization in January 2011. Net cash generated from investing activities resulted primarily from the utilization of restricted cash generated from the AIA initial public offering and ALICO sale and the monetization of MetLife securities received in 2010 when ALICO was sold.

Figure 13: Net Cash Flows and Changes in Cash from Operating, Investing, and Financing Activities, from First Quarter 2007 through Fourth Quarter 2011

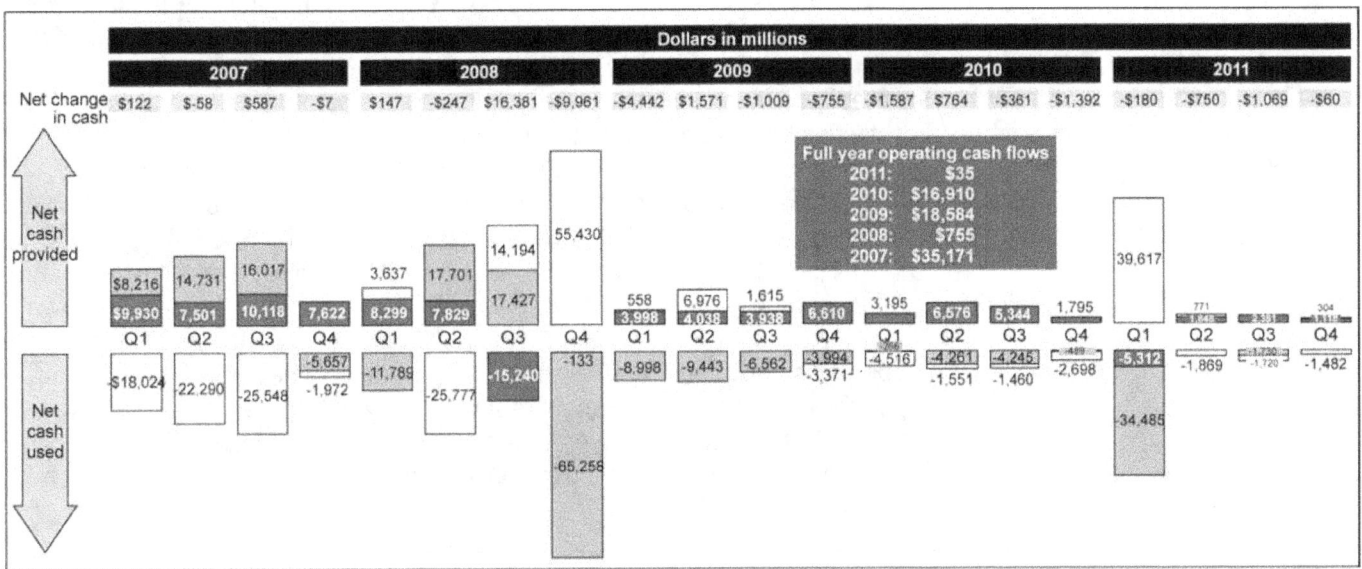

Source: GAO analysis of AIG SEC filings.

Note: Operating cash flows of $755 million for 2008 as originally reported (restated as negative $122 million in AIG's 2010 10K) and $35.171 billion for 2007 include both continuing and discontinued operations as of year-end 2010. Operating cash flows from continuing operations was net cash used of $122 million for 2008 and net cash provided of $32.792 billion for 2007.

AIG's cash flows began to stabilize in 2009 and 2010. Since the third quarter of 2008, quarterly financing cash flows have been negative except for two quarters, reflecting the company's still limited access to the private capital markets. The negative amounts increased over the first three quarters of 2010, but they were much smaller than the negative amounts recorded in the first three quarters of 2009 and decreased significantly in the fourth quarter of 2010.

Throughout 2009 and 2010, AIG had net cash inflows from operating activities and had returned to a precrisis condition of net cash outflows from investing activities—the latter indicating that the company is once again purchasing or expanding its base of income-producing assets rather than selling them to raise cash. AIG reported in its second quarter 2010 10Q filing with SEC that it primarily used its cash flows to meet its debt obligations and the liquidity needs of its subsidiaries. In the first quarter of 2011, AIG's net cash flows diminished primarily due to payments the company made to FRBNY. The company's net cash flows decreased to $5.3 billion for its operating activities, mostly because of a $6.4 billion payment to the FRBNY revolving credit facility and $2 billion in unrealized losses on earnings. However, the company's operating activities benefited from $1.2 billion in net cash flows provided by discontinued operations. AIG's net cash flows also decreased for its financing activities, by nearly $34.5 billion, largely because of $26.4 billion in repayment of the FRBNY SPV preferred interests, $14.6 billion in FRBNY credit facility payments, and $9.1 billion in repayment of Treasury SPV preferred interests, offset in part by $20.3 billion in proceeds drawn on a Treasury's Series F equity facility. In addition, instead of investing in operations or acquiring businesses, the company had $39.6 billion in positive net cash flows from investment activities largely due to $30.5 billion that included activities related to AIG's recapitalization and $4.2 billion from sales of short-term investments.

AIG CDS Premiums Continue to Trend Downward Toward Precrisis Levels

Dropping from their peak in May 2009, AIG CDS premiums have decreased and appear to be trending down generally toward precrisis levels. CDS premiums are the price insured parties pay to purchase CDS protection against AIG defaulting on senior unsecured debt, they are another indicator of AIG's financial strength. This indicator measures what the market believes to be AIG's probability of default by tracking premiums (expressed in basis points) paid by an insured party against a possible default on a senior unsecured bond and the spreads between the 3-year and 5-year premiums.[41] This measure pertains to CDS prices on AIG and not AIGFP's CDS inventory that the company is winding down; it is a composite of what dealers would charge customers for CDS on AIG. Higher basis point levels indicate a higher premium for a CDS contract. The higher the CDS premiums, the greater the market's perception of credit risk associated with AIG. Conversely, the lower the CDS premiums, the greater its confidence in AIG's financial strength (the lower the market's expectation that AIG will default).

---

[41]A basis point is a common measure used in quoting yield on bills, notes, and bonds and represents 1/100 of a percent of yield.

AIG's CDS premiums generally continued to decrease since May 2009, and as of March 8, 2012, were similar to their March 2008 level for the 3-year and 5-year CDS premiums (see fig. 14). From May 2009 through March 2010, the CDS index for the insurance sector declined, but not as much as the CDS premiums for AIG. From March 2010 through May 2011, AIG's CDS premiums declined slightly. The premiums rose somewhat during the latter part of 2011 but receded again in the first 3 months of 2012. While the overall trend is positive, meaning declining premiums, the extent to which this decline in the cost to protect against an AIG default reflects confidence in the stand-alone creditworthiness of AIG or relative to the extent to which the decline is due to the ongoing federal assistance to AIG is unclear. As the Federal Reserve has noted, the premium on AIG's CDS is based both on the market's assessment of the government's level of commitment to assist AIG and AIG's financial strength.

Figure 14: AIG CDS Premiums on AIG, January 2007 through March 2012

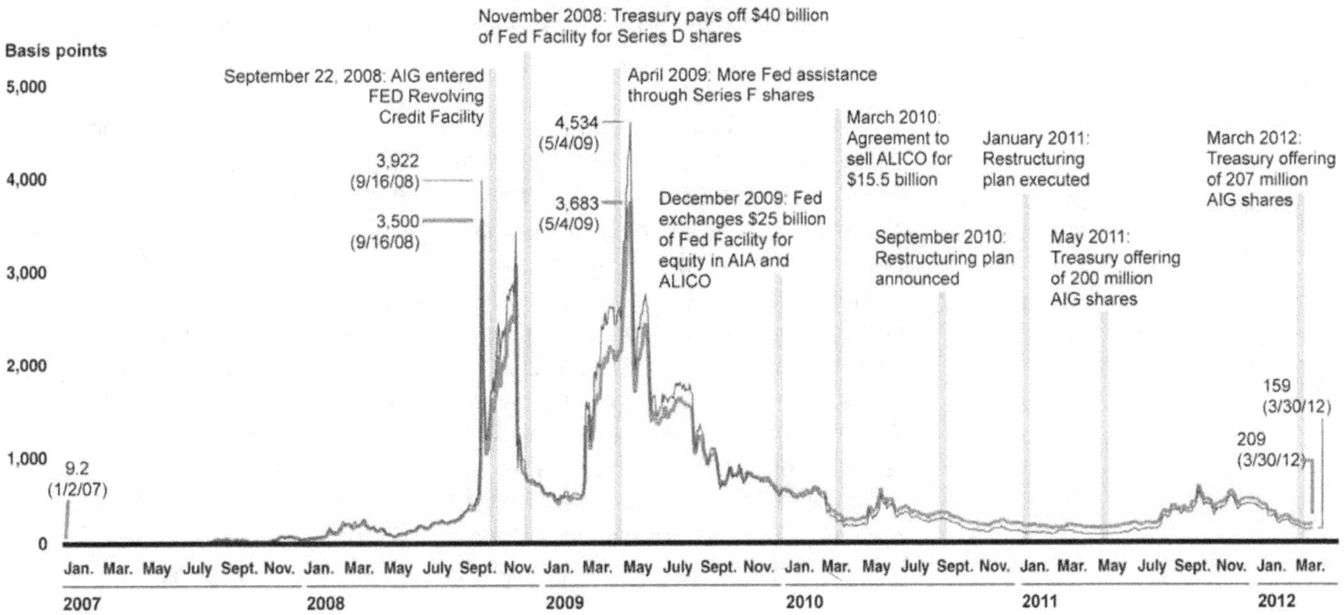

Source: GAO analysis of Thomson Reuters Datastream.

Note: CDS provide protection to the buyer of the CDS contract if the assets covered by the contract go into default.

AIG's Credit Ratings Have Remained Stable since the First Quarter of 2011

Ratings of AIG's debt and financial strength by various credit rating agencies showed mixed trends in the first quarter of 2011, but since then they have remained stable. Credit ratings measure a company's ability to repay its obligations and directly affect that company's cost of and ability to access unsecured financing. If a company's ratings are downgraded, its borrowing costs can increase, capital can be more difficult to raise, business partners may terminate contracts or transactions, counterparties can demand additional collateral, and operations can become more constrained generally. Rating agencies can downgrade a company's key credit ratings if they believe it is unable to meet its obligations. In AIG's case, downgrades could affect its ability to raise funds and could increase the cost of financing its major insurance operations. Downgrades in AIG's credit ratings also could result in downgrades on insurer financial strength ratings for the AIG life and property/casualty companies, further declines in credit limits, and counterparties demanding that AIG post additional collateral. Collectively, these effects could impede AIG's restructuring efforts and hamper any plans to access traditional sources of private capital to replace the public investments. Conversely, an upgrade in AIG's credit ratings would indicate an improvement in its condition and possibly lead to lower borrowing costs and facilitate corporate restructuring.

Several of AIG's key credit ratings remained fairly stable during the last three quarters of 2010, became mixed in the first quarter of 2011, and have since stabilized and remained stable through the end of 2011.[42] Since our last report on AIG insurance sector ratings, S&P, Moody's and Fitch Ratings have not reported any changes to their ratings of AIG's long-term or short-term debt, nor have these agencies or AM Best changed their ratings of AIG's property/casualty financial strength ratings. However, on January 27, 2012, AM Best revised their ratings outlook for AIG's life insurer and property/casualty lines from "negative" to "stable." According to the rating agency, the revised outlook for AIG's life lines reflects improved surrender rates, strong positive cash flows, and the progress made to restore its leading market positions.[43] The stable outlook reflects Chartis's U.S. market position; its ability to lead underwrite, attract, and retain clients by leveraging its significant global

---

[42]See appendix II for a detailed listing of AIG's historical and current credit ratings and an explanation of the meaning of the various credit ratings.

[43]"Surrender rates" refer to the extent that customers are 'cashing-in' the value of their policy, which results in a cash outflow for the life insurance company.

capacity, extensive product offerings, and innovation; and greater emphasis on pricing premiums to match the chance that clients will make an insurance claim and using data-based models to determine insurance premiums. It also suggests that estimates of their claim obligations compares to earlier projections will be acceptable, and Chartis will continue to maintain a supportive level of risk-adjusted capitalization through favorable net earnings while providing shareholder dividends to its parent in accordance with historical norms. The stable outlook also reflects continued improvements at AIG including the January 2011 implementation of the company's recapitalization plan, AIG's recent issuance of debt and equity in the public capital markets, enhanced holding company liquidity and the orderly wind down of AIGFP. Only Fitch Ratings has reported any rating change for AIG's life insurer financial strength rating, and this change was a rating upgrade, from A-/stable to A/stable on April 25, 2011.

AIG's Property/Casualty Companies Were Profitable throughout 2010 and 2011 Because Investment Income More than Offset Underwriting Losses

To track the performance of AIG's insurance companies, we use an indicator of AIG's underwriting ratios. In nearly every quarter since the first quarter of 2008, underwriting in AIG's property/casualty companies has not been profitable, but net income generally has been positive because investment income more than offset underwriting losses. For property/casualty insurers, underwriting profitability can be measured using the combined ratio, which is the sum of the loss and the expense ratios. The loss ratio measures claims costs plus claims adjustment expenses relative to net earned premiums. For example, a loss ratio of 77.3 percent indicates that 77.3 cents of every dollar in premiums earned are used for claims and claims-related costs. A rising loss ratio indicates rising claims costs relative to the premiums earned, which may be due to increased claims losses, decreased premiums earned, or a combination of the two. The expense ratio measures the level of underwriting administrative expenses relative to net premiums earned and is a measure of underwriting efficiency. For example, an expense ratio of 22.4 percent indicates that 22.4 cents of every dollar in premiums earned are used for underwriting expenses. The combined ratio (combining the loss ratio and the expense ratio) is an overall measure of a property/casualty insurer's underwriting profitability. Thus, a combined ratio of less than 100 percent would indicate that an insurer's underwriting is profitable and a ratio of more than 100 percent would indicate an underwriting loss.

Our indicator tracks AIG's underwriting ratios quarterly compared with the average underwriting ratios of its 15 property/casualty insurance peers or competitors and AIG's investment income and net income as percentages of premiums earned. To identify the 15 property/casualty insurance peers of AIG, we analyzed the distributions of 2009 direct premiums written (DPW) by lines of business of 30 property/casualty companies that each had more than $1 billion in DPW for 2009.[44] From these companies, we defined a "peer" of AIG as a company that generated more than 90 percent of its DPW in lines that accounted for more than 60 percent of AIG's DPW. We defined a nonpeer of AIG as a company that generated more than 80 percent of its DPW in lines that accounted for less than 40 percent of AIG's DPW or more than 50 percent of its DPW in a single line that was less than 20 percent of AIG's DPW.

The top panel of figure 15 compares AIG's ratios to those of its peers. Since 2007, which was just prior to the onset of federal assistance to AIG, AIG's combined ratios usually have been higher than the average of its peers. Nevertheless, since the first quarter of 2010—with the exception of the third quarter of 2010 when the combined ratios of AIG's peers averaged 99.7 (a ratio of less than 100 indicates that the underwriting was profitable)—the combined ratios for AIG and its peers have exceeded 100, indicating that their underwriting usually has not been profitable. By comparison, in 2007 the underwriting of both AIG and its peers were profitable. From 2008 through 2009 underwriting remained profitable for AIG peers but became unprofitable for AIG. The top panel of the figure also shows that while AIG's expense ratios have been lower than the average of its peers in every quarter, its loss ratios have been

[44]We reviewed 30 property/casualty companies and identified 15 as AIG's property/casualty insurance peers based on the similarities in the distributions of their premiums written in 2009 by lines of business. As did AIG, these companies wrote premiums in several property/casualty lines of insurance. The companies are ACE, Allegheny, Allianz SE, American Financial, Arch Capital, Argo Group, Chubb, CNA, Fairfax Financial, Hartford Financial Services, Liberty Mutual, Markel, Old Republic, Travelers, and WR Berkley. Other property/casualty insurers not identified as peers were mostly companies concentrated in private auto insurance or home/farm owners insurance and other lines of insurance that were not major lines for AIG. These companies are Allstate; Assurant, Inc.; Bank of America; Berkshire Hathaway (GEICO); Erie Insurance Group; FM Global; Nationwide Mutual; Progressive; QBE Insurance Group; State Farm Fire and Casualty; State Farm Mutual Auto Insurance; Tokio Marine; United Services Automobile Association; White Mountains; and Zurich Financial Services.

higher than the average of its peers in every quarter.[45] The lower panels of the figure show that despite a combined ratio usually over 100, AIG's property/casualty companies had positive net income in 16 of the 20 quarters because investment income, which increased every quarter in 2011, more than offset the underwriting losses.[46]

[45]Historical operating ratios for commercial insurance have been revised to include Private Client Group and exclude HSB Group, Inc. The loss ratio for the fourth quarter of 2009 includes a $2.3 billion increase in the reserve for prior years' adverse loss development. The underwriting expense for the fourth quarter of 2008 includes a $1.2 billion charge for impairment to goodwill, increasing the expense ratio by 22.5 points. Claims related to major catastrophes were $1.4 billion in 2008, including hurricane claims of $1.1 billion in the third quarter of 2008. Conversely, claims related to major catastrophes were $100 million in 2007.

[46]Investment returns are not considered part of underwriting and thus are not included in the ratios.

Figure 15: Quarterly Statutory Underwriting Ratios of AIG (Chartis Domestic and Foreign Property/Casualty Insurance Companies) Compared to Averages for 15 Peers and AIG's Property/Casualty Investment Income and Net Income as Percentages of Premiums Earned, First Quarter 2007 through Fourth Quarter of 2011

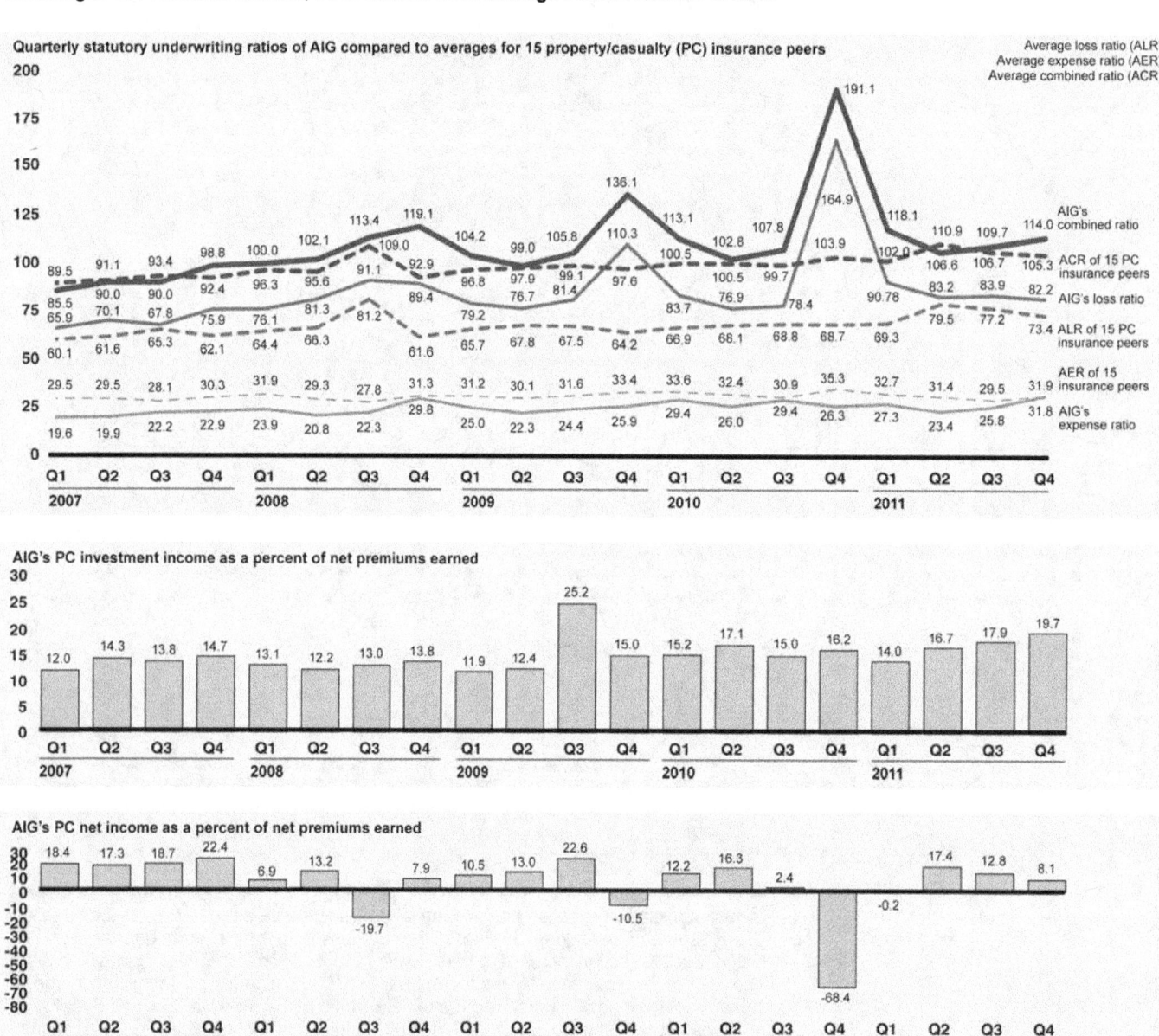

Sources: GAO analysis of AIG and peers data per SNL Financial.

Note: The ratios are originally reported, nonrestated figures. We did not include restated figures because they revise the prior periods to reflect the effect of discontinued operations, acquisitions, or other changes to conform to the current period. We determined AIG's property/casualty peers for our analysis by comparing various property/casualty companies' distribution of premiums written in 2009 by their lines of business. Similar to AIG, its peers have several lines of business. The 15 peers are ACE, Alleghany, Allianz SE, American Financial, Arch Capital, Argo Group, Chubb, CNA, Fairfax Financial, Hartford, L berty Mutual, Markel, Old Republic, Travelers, and WR Berkley. Other property/casualty companies were not included in the peer group for this analysis. Most of these companies were concentrated either in the private auto insurance business or home/farm owners insurance, neither of which is among AIG's largest lines of business. These companies are Allstate; Assurant, Inc.; Bank of America; Berkshire Hathaway (GEICO); Erie Insurance Group; FM Global; Nationwide Mutual; Progressive; QBE Insurance Group; State Farm Fire and Casualty; State Farm Mutual Auto Insurance; Tokio Marine; United Services Automobile Association; White Mountains; and Zurich Financial Services.

While our data cover only 5 full calendar years, they suggest a pattern of loss ratios increasing overall and being volatile at times and expense ratios that have remained fairly stable. Investment returns were high enough for AIG to be profitable in 8 of the 12 quarters from 2007 through 2009, and 6 of the 8 quarters through the end of 2011. The capital losses in the fourth quarter of 2010 (68.4 percent) largely reflect a $3.7 billion fourth quarter loss in AIG's property/casualty net income. Moreover, in the fourth quarter of 2010, AIG's combined ratio increased sharply to 191.1, while the average ratio of its peers rose modestly to 103.9. The sharp increase for AIG resulted primarily from domestic property/casualty insurance in which claims and claims adjustment expenses rose 105 percent and underwriting expenses rose 31 percent, while premiums earned declined 4 percent. Second, the 4 percent rise in premiums earned by foreign property/casualty insurance was more than offset by increases of 30 percent in claims and claims adjustment expenses and 19 percent in underwriting expenses. Claims and claims adjustment expenses increased mostly from actual losses exceeding estimated losses (adverse loss development) that was recognized and recorded in 2010 for asbestos and excess casualty and workers' compensation coverage in years prior to 2010. Increased underwriting expenses reflect increased costs in areas such as brokers' commissions, employee incentive programs, marketing, financial systems, impairments of intangible assets, divestitures, and workforce reductions.[47] However, in the first quarter of 2011, the loss ratio and combined ratio declined considerably from the fourth quarter of 2010 due to declines in claims and claims-adjustment expenses and remained lower throughout 2011, with no adverse loss development reported in the fourth quarter of 2011.

---

[47]An impairment to an intangible asset is a decline in its fair value or expected future cash flows that is recognized by reducing the asset's value that is carried on the books.

Since our last report in July 2011, much of the federal assistance to benefit AIG has been repaid by or on behalf of AIG. Debt assistance through Maiden Lane II has been repaid, as has equity assistance through the AIA SPV. The remaining federal assistance to AIG consists of remaining assets and accrued interest in Maiden Lane III and remaining Treasury-owned common shares in AIG to be sold. With sales of AIG common stock thus far, Treasury has reduced its equity interest in AIG from 77 percent to 70 percent. However, monitoring the markets to identify divestment strategies that will strike the right balance between Treasury's competing goals of maximizing taxpayers' returns and exiting its investments as soon as practicable will remain important for Treasury. Consequently, the government's, and thus the taxpayers', exposure to AIG will be tied to the success and ongoing performance of AIG. The sustainability of any positive trends in AIG's operations will depend on how well it manages its business in the current economic environment. Similarly, the government's ability to fully recoup its assistance will be determined by the long-term health of AIG as well as other market factors that are beyond the control of AIG or the government such as the performance of the insurance sectors, the credit derivatives markets, and investors' interest in the company—including large institutional investors. We will continue to monitor these issues in our future work.

Agency Comments

We provided a draft of this report to Treasury for review and comment. Treasury did not provide overall written comments. We also shared a draft of this report with the Federal Reserve and AIG. We received written technical comments from Treasury, the Federal Reserve, and AIG, which we have incorporated in the report as appropriate.

We are sending copies of this report to appropriate congressional committees, the Financial Stability Oversight Board, the Special Inspector General for TARP, the Department of the Treasury, the federal banking regulators, and other interested parties. In addition, the report also is available at no charge on the GAO website at http://www.gao.gov.

If you or your staffs have any questions concerning this report please contact Lawrance L. Evans, Jr. at (202) 512-4802 or evansl@gao.gov. Contact points for our Offices of Congressional Relations and Public Affairs may be found on the last page of this report. GAO staff who made major contributions to this report are listed in appendix III.

Lawrance L. Evans, Jr.
Acting Director
Financial Markets and
    Community Investment

List of Congressional Committees

The Honorable Daniel K. Inouye
Chairman
The Honorable Thad Cochran
Vice Chairman
Committee on Appropriations
United States Senate

The Honorable Tim Johnson
Chairman
The Honorable Richard C. Shelby
Ranking Member
Committee on Banking, Housing,
And Urban Affairs
United States Senate

The Honorable Kent Conrad
Chairman
The Honorable Jeff Sessions
Ranking Member
Committee on the Budget
United States Senate

The Honorable Max Baucus
Chairman
The Honorable Orrin G. Hatch
Ranking Member
Committee on Finance
United States Senate

The Honorable Hal Rogers
Chairman
The Honorable Norm Dicks
Ranking Member
Committee on Appropriations
House of Representatives

The Honorable Paul Ryan
Chairman
The Honorable Chris Van Hollen
Ranking Member
Committee on the Budget
House of Representatives

The Honorable Spencer Bachus
Chairman
The Honorable Barney Frank
Ranking Member
Committee on Financial Services
House of Representatives

The Honorable Dave Camp
Chairman
The Honorable Sander Levin
Ranking Member
Committee on Ways and Means
House of Representative

Appendix I: Maiden Lane II Asset Auctions

To repay the Federal Reserve Bank of New York (FRBNY), in early April 2011, FRBNY began offering segments of the Maiden Lane II residential mortgage-backed securities (RMBS) portfolio for sale to a group of dealers on a more or less weekly basis through early June 2011, a strategy that it hoped would avoid market disruption. Following an offer by American International Group, Inc. (AIG) to repurchase the assets it had sold to Maiden Lane II, FRBNY announced on March 30, 2011, that it had declined AIG's offer. FRBNY and the Board of Governors of the Federal Reserve System said this was done to serve the public interest of maximizing returns from any sale and promoting financial stability. In light of improved conditions in the RMBS market and a high level of interest, FRBNY stated that it would begin more extensive asset sales through a competitive sales process. FRBNY's investment manager, BlackRock Solutions, disposed of the Maiden Lane II securities through a competitive sales process. To maximize returns to the public, FRBNY did not stipulate a time frame for disposing of these assets. Through June 9, 2011, Maiden Lane II held several auctions and sold nearly $10 billion from its portfolio (see table 5). In addition, on January 19, 2012, FRBNY announced that it had sold assets with a current face value of $7 billion through a competitive process to Credit Suisse Securities (USA) LLC and on February 8, 2012, it announced that it sold assets with a current face value of $6.2 billion through a competitive process to Goldman Sachs & Co. According to FRBNY, the proceeds from both sales would enable the repayment of the entire remaining outstanding balance of the FRBNY loan to the Maiden Lane II in early March 2012. More recently, on February 28, 2012, FRBNY announced the sale of the remaining securities in the Maiden Lane II portfolio, and as of March 7, 2012, the facility had repaid FRBNY the outstanding principal and interest.

Table 5: Dates and Values of Maiden Lane II Asset Auctions, April 6, 2011, through February 28, 2012

Date of auction	Face value of assets sold[a]	Cumulative assets sold (face value)
April 6, 2011	$1,326,856,873	$1,326,856,873
April 13, 2011	626,080,072	1,952,936,945
April 14, 2011	534,127,946	2,487,064,891
April 28, 2011	1,122,794,209	3,609,859,100
May 4, 2011	1,773,371,055	5,383,230,155
May 10, 2011	427,486,898	5,810,717,053
May 12, 2011	1,373,506,029	7,184,223,082
May 19, 2011	878,641,682	8,062,864,764

Date of auction	Face value of assets sold[a]	Cumulative assets sold (face value)
June 9, 2011	1,898,594,878	9,961,459,642
January 19, 2012[b]	7,014,000,000	16,975,459,642
February 8, 2012[b]	6,200,000,000	23,175,459,642
February 28, 2012	6,000,000,000	29,175,459,642
Total	**$29,175,459,642**	

Source: GAO analysis of FRBNY data.

Note: There were no asset auctions for Maiden Lane II from mid-June 2011 through mid-January 2012.

[a]Value is the face amount of the most recent balance of principal outstanding.

[b]On January 19, 2012, FRBNY announced that it sold assets with a current face value of $7.014 billion through a competitive process to Credit Suisse Securities (USA) LLC and on February 8, 2012, it announced that it sold assets with a current face value of $6.2 billion through a competitive process to Goldman Sachs & Co. On February 28, 2012, FRBNY announced the sale of the remaining securities in the Maiden Lane II portfolio with the sale of assets with a current face amount of $6 billion through a competitive process to Credit Suisse Securities (USA) LLC, As of March 21, 2012, in addition to the facility having repaid FRBNY the outstanding principal and interest, had no deferred payment and interest payable to subsidiaries of AIG had been reduced to zero and the SPV had net portfolio holdings of only $19 million. The management of the portfolio generated a net gain for the benefit of the public of approximately $2.8 billion, including $580 million in accrued interest on the FRBNY loan.

Appendix II: Overview of Definitions of Credit Ratings and AIG's Credit Ratings

Credit ratings measure a company's ability to repay its obligations and directly affect that company's cost of and ability to access unsecured financing. If a company's ratings are downgraded, its borrowing costs can increase, capital can be more difficult to raise, business partners may terminate contracts or transactions, counterparties can demand additional collateral, and operations can become more constrained generally. Rating agencies can downgrade the company's key credit ratings if they believe the company is unable to meet its obligations. In American International Group, Inc.'s (AIG) case, this could affect its ability to raise funds and increase the cost of financing its major insurance operations, and, in turn, impede AIG's restructuring efforts. Conversely, an upgrade in AIG's credit ratings would indicate an improvement in its condition and possibly lead to lower borrowing costs and facilitate corporate restructuring.

Moody's Investors Service (Moody's), Standard and Poor's (S&P), and Fitch Ratings (Fitch) are three of the credit rating agencies that assess the creditworthiness of AIG. Each of the rating agencies uses a unique rating to denote the grade and quality of the bonds being rated. Table 6 provides an overview of the ratings for Moody's, S&P, and Fitch.

Table 6: Summary of Rating Agencies' Ratings

Grade and quality	Definitions	Moody's[a]	S&P[b]	Fitch[b]
Highest grade and quality	There is an extremely strong capacity to meet financial commitments on the obligation and bonds have little investment risk.	Aaa	AAA	AAA
High grade and quality	There is a very strong capacity to meet financial commitment on the obligation and bonds have very little investment risk, but margins of protection may be lower than with the highest grade bonds.	Aa	AA	AA
Upper-medium grade and quality	There is a strong capacity to meet financial commitment on the obligation and the principal and interest are adequately secured, but the bonds are more vulnerable to a changing economy.	A	A	A
Medium and lower-medium grade	There are adequate protections for these obligations, but the bonds have investment and speculative characteristics. This group comprises the lowest level of investment grade bonds.	Baa	BBB	BBB
Noninvestment and speculative grades	There is little protection on these obligations and the interest and principal may be in danger, in cases in which default may be likely.	Ba1 and below	BB+ and below	BB+ and below

Sources: GAO descriptions of information from Moody's, S&P, and Fitch.

[a]Moody's has numerical modifiers of 1, 2, and 3 in each rating classification from Aa to B: "1" indicates that the issue ranks in the higher end of the category, "2" indicates a midrange ranking, and "3" indicates that the issue ranks in the lower end of the category.

[b]S&P and Fitch: Ratings from 'AA' to 'CCC' may be modified by the addition of a plus (+) or minus (-) sign to show relative standing within the major rating categories.

As shown in table 7, AIG's key credit ratings remained largely unchanged from May 2009 through December 2011, primarily because federal assistance provided AIG with needed liquidity. From March 31, 2009, to December 15, 2009, AM Best, Moody's, and S&P maintained the same credit ratings for AIG's long-term debt and the financial strength of its property/casualty and life insurance companies due in large part to support that the Federal Reserve and Treasury provided.[1] Since we last reported on the insurance ratings, S&P, Moody's, and Fitch have not reported any changes to their ratings of AIG's long-term or short-term debt. Nor have these agencies or AM Best changed their ratings of AIG's property/casualty financial strength ratings. However, on January 27, 2012, AM Best revised their ratings outlook for AIG's life insurer and property/casualty lines from "negative" to "stable." According to the rating agency, the revised outlook for AIG's life lines reflects improved surrender rates, strong positive cash flows, and the progress made to restore its leading market positions. This stable outlook also reflects Chartis's U.S. market position; its ability to lead, attract and retain clients by leveraging its significant global capacity, extensive product offerings and innovation; and greater emphasis on technical pricing and predictive modeling. It further suggests that any future reserve development will be acceptable, that Chartis will continue to maintain a supportive level of risk-adjusted capitalization through favorable net earnings while providing shareholder dividends to its parent in accordance with historical norms. This stable outlook also reflects continued improvements at AIG including the January 2011 implementation of the company's recapitalization plan, AIG's recent issuance of debt and equity in the public capital markets, enhanced holding company liquidity and the orderly wind down of AIGFP. Only Fitch has reported any rating change for AIG's life insurer financial strength rating, and this change was a rating upgrade, from A-/stable to A/stable on April 25, 2011.

---

[1] AIG's long-term debt was rated at A-/Negative (S&P) and A3/Negative (Moody's), and its short-term debt was rated at A-1 (S&P) and P-1 (Moody's). While these ratings are described using slightly different terminology, they tend to show relative consistency in the strength of AIG's debt.

Table 7: AIG's Key Credit Ratings, March 31, 2009, through December 31, 2011

Rating agency	Mar. 31, 2009	May 15, 2009	Dec. 15, 2009	Mar. 31, 2010	July 31, 2010	Sep. 30, 2010	Dec. 31, 2010	Mar. 31, 2011	July 31, 2011	Dec. 31, 2011
Debt										
Long-term										
Potential consequences of a future downgrade	AIGFP would have to post collateral and termination payments. The total obligations depend on the market and other factors at the time of the downgrade. For example: At December 31, 2011, a one-notch downgrade from S&P would have resulted in negligible additional collateral postings and termination payments, while a one-notch downgrade from Moody's and a two-notch from S&P would increase that cost to $264 million. Another notch downgrade would have increased that cost to $531 million. By comparison, at June 30, 2010, a one-notch, two-notch, or three-notch downgrade from S&P and Moody's would have cost AIG negligibly and up to $298 million, and $650 million, respectively, in cumulative additional collateral postings and termination payments.									
S&P	A-/n[a]	n/c	n/c	n/c	n/c	n/c	n/c	A-/s	n/c	n/c
Moody's	A3/n[a]	n/c	n/c	n/c	n/c	n/c	n/c	Baa1/s	n/c	n/c
Fitch	A	BBB/e	n/c	n/c	BBB/s	n/c	n/c	n/c	n/c	n/c
Short-term										
Potential consequences of a future downgrade	According to AIG, currently the company does not issue commercial paper or other short term debt instruments. Therefore, there would be no immediate financial impact if there was a downgrade of its short term ratings. Current credit facility pricing is tied to the long-term ratings.									
S&P	A-1 for AIG Funding, Curzon, and Nightingale[a]	n/c	n/c	n/c	n/c	n/c	n/c	A-2	n/c	n/c
Moody's	P-1 for AIG Funding[a]	n/c	n/c	n/c	n/c	on review for possible downgrade	n/c	P-2/s	n/c	n/c
Fitch	F1	n/c	n/c	n/c	n/c	n/c	affirmed and withdrawn Nov. 19, 2010	not rated	n/c	n/c
Financial strength										
Life insurer										

Rating agency	Mar. 31, 2009	May 15, 2009	Dec. 15, 2009	Mar. 31, 2010	July 31, 2010	Sep. 30, 2010	Dec. 31, 2010	Mar. 31, 2011	July 31, 2011	Dec. 31, 2011
Potential consequences of a future downgrade	According to AIG, a ratings downgrade of SAFG Retirement Services Inc., would have a significant negative impact. AIG's domestic life insurance new business would be severely impacted, in several instances forcing the company to exit businesses that serve either the high-net-worth marketplace or businesses that are governed by trust contracts including universal life, structured settlements, pensions and private placements. The company would need to continue to dedicate key resources to retention and management of existing producer and client relationships. Additional retention strategies would need to be implemented.										
	AIG's retirement services businesses would also be highly impacted since the companies distribute through rating sensitive distribution channels. There is a minimum rating that many banks or groups cannot go below and a further downgrade would certainly result in the companies falling below that minimum. With respect to variable annuities, a further ratings downgrade could cause a significant number of major firms to resuspend sales or to initiate permanent suspension, which would increase surrender rates and, potentially foster partial withdrawals that lock-in adverse death benefit exposures, and result in a significant loss of wholesalers.										
AM Best	A/n[a]	n/c	n/c	n/c	n/c	n/c	n/c	n/c	n/c	n/c
S&P	A+/n	n/c	n/c	n/c	n/c	n/c	n/c	A+/s	n/c	n/c
Moody's	A1/developing	n/c	n/c	A1/n	n/c	n/c	n/c	A2/s	n/c	n/c
Fitch	AA-	A-/e	n/c	n/c	A-/s	n/c	n/c	n/c	A/s	n/c
Property/casualty insurer			n/c	n/c						
Potential consequences of a future downgrade	According to AIG, a further downgrade of Chartis's financial strength rating from a leading rating agency could, in the extreme, irreparably harm Chartis's worldwide businesses, potentially putting Chartis into "run-off", meaning that it could only service business left with the company as it could not effectively write profitable, new business. In the U.S., AM Best is the key rating agency for Chartis's U.S. businesses, while Standard & Poor's ratings have greater impact on a global scale. A further degradation of either of these ratings could effectively put Chartis at a severe competitive disadvantage.										
	Prior to September 2008, AIG's credit ratings and financial position were advantageous for its property casualty companies and provided an uplift in the insurance operations ratings. Since 2008, AIG's financial challenges have put downward pressure on Chartis's financial strength ratings to the point that financial strength is no longer a key competitive advantage for Chartis as most of its key competitors have stronger ratings.										
AM Best	A/n[a]	n/c	n/c	n/c	n/c	n/c	n/c	n/c	n/c	n/c
S&P	A+/n	n/c	n/c	n/c	n/c	n/c	n/c	A/s	n/c	n/c
Moody's	Aa3/n	n/c	n/c	n/c	n/c	n/c	n/c	A1/s	n/c	n/c
Fitch	AA-	A+/e	n/c	placed rating on rating watch - negative	A+/s	n/c	n/c	A/s	n/c	n/c

Sources: GAO description of information from AIG Securities and Exchange Commission filings; S&P, Fitch, Moody's, and AM Best; and AIG.

Note: N/c means no change, n means negative, e means evolving, and s means stable.

[a]These are key ratings.

Appendix III: GAO Contact and Staff Acknowledgments

GAO Contact	Lawrance L. Evans, Jr., (202) 512-4802 or evansl@gao.gov
Staff Acknowledgments	In addition to the contact named above, Karen Tremba (Assistant Director), Rachel DeMarcus, John Forrester, Marc Molino, Patricia Moye, Jennifer Schwartz, and Melvin Thomas made important contributions to this report.

Appendix IV: Glossary of Terms

Adjusted Basis	The net cost of an asset or security that is used to compute the gains or losses on that asset or security. It is calculated by starting with the original cost of an asset or security, then adding the value of any improvements, legal fees, and assessments and subtracting the value of any accumulated depreciation, amortization, and other losses.
Asset	An item owned by an individual, corporation, or government that provides a benefit, has economic value, and could be converted into cash. For businesses, an asset generates cash flow and may include, for example, accounts receivable and inventory. Assets are listed on a company's balance sheet.
Book	A trader's record or inventory of long (buy) and short (sell) positions on securities it holds and orders placed. A book may hold few or several positions and a trader may have several books, which are variously organized, such as by types of product or risk.
Capital	The value of cash, goods, and other financial resources a business uses to generate income or make an investment. Companies can raise capital from investors by selling stocks and bonds. Capital is often used to measure the financial strength of a company.
Capital Market	The market for long-term funds in which securities such as common stock, preferred stock, and bonds are traded. Both the primary market for new issues and the secondary market for existing securities are part of the capital market.
Claims (Adjustment) Expenses	Costs of adjusting a claim that include attorneys' fees and investigation expenses.
Collateral	Properties or other assets pledged by a borrower to secure credit from a lender. If the borrower does not pay back or defaults on the loan, the lender may seize the collateral.

Collateralized Debt Obligation	Securities backed by a pool of bonds, loans, or other assets. In a basic collateralized debt obligation, a pool of bonds, loans, or other assets are pooled and securities then are issued in different tranches (see "tranche" and "mezzanine tranche") that vary in risk and return.
Combined Ratio	This ratio is a common measure of the performance of the daily operations of an insurance company. It is calculated by adding the amount of incurred losses and the amount of expenses incurred by the company and dividing that combined amount by the earned premium generated during the same period. The ratio describes the related cost of losses and expenses for every $100 of earned premiums. A ratio of less than 100 percent generally indicates that the company is making underwriting profit while a ratio of more than 100 percent generally means that it is paying out more money in claims that it is receiving from premiums.
Commercial Paper	An unsecured obligation with maturities ranging from 2 to 270 days issued by banks, corporations, and other borrowers with high credit ratings to finance short-term credit needs, such as operating expenses and account receivables. Commercial paper is a low-cost alternative to bank loans. Issuing commercial paper allows a company to raise large amounts of funds quickly without the need to register with the Securities and Exchange Commission, either by selling them directly to an investor or to a dealer who then sells them to a large and varied pool of institutional buyers.
Credit Default Swap	Bilateral contracts that are sold over the counter and transfer credit risks from one party to another. In return for a periodic fee, the seller (who is offering credit protection) agrees to compensate the buyer (who is buying credit protection) if a specified credit event, such as default, occurs.
Derivative	A financial instrument, traded on- or off-exchange, the price of which directly depends on the value of one or more underlying commodities. Derivatives involve the trading of rights or obligations on the basis of the underlying product, but they do not directly transfer property.

Directors and Officer Liability Insurance	Provides coverage when a director or officer of a company commits a negligent act or misleading statement that results in the company being sued.
Equity	Ownership interest in a business in the form of common stock or preferred stock.
Errors and Omissions Liability Insurance (or Coverage)	Insurance protection to various professions for negligent acts or omissions resulting in bodily injury, property damage, or liability to a client.
Expense Ratio	The ratio of underwriting expenses to net premiums earned. It is a measure of underwriting efficiency, in which an increase in the ratio represents increased expenses relative to premiums. The underwriting expenses include the amortization of deferred policy acquisition costs (commissions, taxes, licenses and fees, and other underwriting expenses amortized over the policy term), and insurance operating costs and expenses. For example, a 22.4 expense ratio indicates that 22.4 cents out of every dollar in premiums earned are used for underwriting expenses.
Fair Value	An estimated value of an asset or liability that is reasonable to all willing parties involved in a transaction taking into account market conditions other than liquidation. For example, the fair value of derivative liability represents the fair market valuation of the liabilities in a portfolio of derivatives. In this example, the fair value provides an indicator of the dollar amount the market thinks the trader of the portfolio would need to pay to eliminate its liabilities.
Goodwill (and Goodwill Impairment)	Goodwill occurs when a company buys another entity and pays more than the market value of all assets on the entity's books. A company will pay more because of intangibles—such trademarks and copyrights—on the books at historical cost and other factors—such as human capital, brand name, and client base—that accounting conventions do not capture on the books. If the company later determines that the entity has lost value and recovery is not a realistic expectation it might decide to record the lost value as an impairment.

Liability	A business's financial obligation that must be made to satisfy the contractual terms of such an obligation. Current liabilities, such as accounts payable or wages, are debts payable within 1 year, while long-term liabilities, such as leases and bond repayments, are payable over a longer period.
Liquidity	Measure of the extent to which a business has cash to meet its immediate and short-term obligations. Liquidity also is measured in terms of a company's ability to borrow money to meet short-term demands for funds.
Loss Ratio	The ratio of claims and claims adjustment expenses incurred to net earned premiums. For example, a 77.3 loss ratio indicates that 77.3 cents out of every dollar in premiums earned are used to adjust and pay claims.
Mezzanine Tranche	A tranche is a piece or portion of a structured deal, or one of several related securities that are issued together but offer different risk-reward characteristics. The mezzanine tranche is subordinated to the senior tranche, but is senior to the equity tranche. The senior tranche is the least-risky tranche whereas the equity tranche is the first loss and riskiest tranche.
Mortgage-Backed Securities	Securities or debt obligations that represent claims to the cash flows from pools of mortgage loans, such as mortgages on residential property. These securities are issued by Ginnie Mae, Fannie Mae, and Freddie Mac, as well as private institutions, such as brokerage firms and banks.
Notional Amount (Gross and Net)	The amount upon which payments between parties to certain types of derivatives contracts are based. The gross notional amount is not exchanged between the parties, but instead represents the underlying quantity upon which payment obligations are computed. The net notional amount represents the maximum dollar level exposure for the portfolio.
Paid-in Capital	Funds provided by investors in exchange for common or preferred stock. Paid-in capital represents the funds raised by the business from equity, and not from ongoing operations.

Preferred Stock (Cumulative, Noncumulative, etc.)	A class of ownership in a corporation or stock that has characteristics of both common stock and debt. Preferred shareholders receive their dividends before common stockholders, but they generally do not have the voting rights available to common stockholders.
Retained Earnings	A calculation of the accumulated earnings of a corporation minus cash dividends since inception.
Reverse Stock Split	A proportionate decrease in the number of shares held by stockholders that a company generally institutes to increase the market price per share of its stock. In a 1-for-10 stock split stockholders would own 1 share for every 10 shares that they owned before the reverse split.
Risk-Based Capital (Insurance)	The amount of required capital that an insurance company must maintain based on the inherent risks in the insurer's operations. Authorized control level risk-based capital is the level at which an insurance commissioner can first take control of an insurance company.
Secured	Secured debt is backed or secured by a pledge of collateral.
Securitization	The process of pooling debt obligations and dividing that pool into portions (called tranches) that can be sold as securities in the secondary market—a market in which investors purchase securities or assets from other investors. Financial institutions use securitization to transfer the credit risk of the assets they originate from their balance sheets to those of the investors who purchased the securities.
Shareholders' Equity	Total assets minus total liabilities of a company, as found on a company's balance sheet. Shareholders' equity is also known as owner's equity, net worth, or book value. The two sources for shareholders' equity are money that originally was invested in the company, along with additional investments made thereafter, and retained earnings.
Soft Market	A market in which supply exceeds demand resulting in a lowering of prices in that market. Also refers to a buyer's market, as buyers hold much of the power in negotiating prices.

Solvency	Minimum standard of financial health for an insurance company, in which assets exceed liabilities. In general, a solvent company is able to pay its debt obligations as they come due.
Special Purpose Vehicle	A legal entity, such as a limited partnership that a company creates to carry out some specific financial purpose or activity. Special purpose vehicles can be used for purposes such as securitizing loans to help spread the credit and interest rate risk of their portfolios over a number of investors.
Trading Position	The amount of a security or commodity owned by an investor or a dealer.
Tranche	A tranche is a portion or class of a security. A security may have several tranches, each with different risks and rates of return, among other differences.
Treasury Stock	Previously issued shares of a company that the company has repurchased from investors.
Unrealized Gains and Losses	A profit or loss on an investment that has not been sold. That is, an unrealized profit or loss occurs when the current price of a security that still is owned by the holder is higher or lower than the price the holder paid for it.
Unsecured Debt	Unsecured debt is not backed by any pledge of collateral.
Warrant	An options contract on an underlying asset that is in the form of a transferable security. A warrant gives the holder the right to purchase a specified amount of the issuer's securities in the future at a specific price.